# We'd Rather Be Writing

## 88 Authors Share Timesaving Dinner Recipes and Other Tips

EDITED BY LOIS WINSTON

*We'd Rather Be Writing: 88 Authors Share Timesaving Dinner Recipes and Other Tips* copyright 2015 by Lois Winston.

This book is a compilation of recipes and timesaving tips contributed by the various authors represented in this book. The individual authors retain all copyrights to their contributions.

All rights reserved. Except for contributors' use of their individual submissions, no part of this book may be used or reproduced in any manner whatsoever without written permission except in the case of brief quotations embodied in critical articles and reviews.

All products and company names are trademarks of their respective owners. Use of them does not imply any affiliation with or endorsement by the trademark owners of this cookbook. We just happen to love using their products and hope you do, too!

Cover design by L. Winston

ISBN: 1-940795-34-6
ISBN-13: 978-1-940795-34-8

# CONTENTS

| | |
|---|---|
| Introduction | 1 |
| Meat Recipes | 5 |
| Pasta Recipes | 33 |
| Poultry Recipes | 57 |
| Seafood & Fish Recipes | 93 |
| Soup, Stew, & Chili Recipes | 111 |
| Vegetarian & Miscellaneous Recipes | 141 |
| Cooking Tips | 171 |
| Household Tips | 175 |
| Organizational Tips | 178 |
| Writing Tips | 182 |
| Miscellaneous Tips | 189 |

# ACKNOWLEDGMENTS

A special thank-you to all the authors who participated in this project. It wouldn't have been possible without you.

And extra thanks to Irene Peterson, Donnell Ann Bell, and Melissa Keir for stepping in as proofreaders.

# INTRODUCTION

Contrary to what the general public thinks, most authors would never be able to support themselves from their book sales. That distinction is reserved for a select few with names like King, Patterson, Roberts, and Evanovich. The rest of us hold down day jobs, sometimes more than one. Our writing becomes our second full-time job—or our third or fourth, for those of us who also juggle family responsibilities.

But writers write because we have to. It's in our DNA. Asking us to stop creating stories would be like asking us to stop breathing. The problem for us becomes carving out time to do that writing. Some of us rise early before the rest of our family members; others stay up way past the time everyone else has gone to bed just to type out a few hundred words each night. We write during our lunch hours and on public transportation to and from those day jobs. We scrawl ideas on napkins and scraps of junk mail and sometimes even on the backs of our hands if nothing else is available.

Somehow in-between all our responsibilities we manage to complete our books. We authors are a resourceful bunch. I never realized just how resourceful until I started chatting with other authors about how they carve time out of their lives to write their books. That's when inspiration hit—again.

I say *again* because last year I had an idea for a combination cookbook and advice book. Other authors thought it was a pretty good idea, and the result was *Bake, Love, Write: 105 Authors Share Dessert Recipes and Advice on Love and Writing*. After the publication of that book, many of the participating authors suggested I do a follow-up.

That's when I began thinking about all those ways we find time to write. Thus was born the idea for *We'd Rather Be Writing: 88 Authors Share Timesaving Dinner Recipes and Other Tips*. In this book you'll find easy, nutritious main course recipes that require a minimum of prep time. Many are one-dish meals. For those that aren't, simply add a salad or a cooked vegetable to round out the meal.

The cookbook portion of this book is divided into six chapters—Seafood & Fish; Meat; Pasta; Poultry; Soup, Stew & Chili; and Vegetarian & Miscellaneous. However, as I divided the recipes up into the various categories, I ran into a dilemma. Do I assign the chicken chili recipe to the Poultry chapter or the Soup, Stew & Chili chapter? And what about the tuna pasta recipe? Does it belong with Seafood & Fish or with Pasta? With no clear-cut solution, I tossed a coin. So make sure you check out all the chapters. You never know where you'll find that perfect dinner for a Tuesday night—or any other night of the week.

Although these are all timesaving recipes, if you employ some of our authors' cooking tips, you'll save even more time—time you can spend writing or doing whatever it is you want to do—whether it's spending more quality time with your kids, exercising, reading, gardening, or working at a favorite hobby. We authors aren't the only people craving more time in our hectic lives.

This book also contains tips for saving time in various aspects of your life beyond meal prep. The authors who contributed to this book are a rather creative and resourceful bunch. I've already implemented some of their suggestions, and I'm sure you will, too.

For those of you who are also writers, you'll find a plethora of great ideas to help you organize your writing life and your manuscripts.

Finally, within the pages of *We'd Rather Be Writing: 88 Authors Share Timesaving Dinner Recipes and Other Tips* you'll be introduced to authors who write a wide range of fiction—everything from mystery to romance to speculative fiction to books for children, young adults, and new adults—and some who write nonfiction. Some of the authors write sweet; others write steamy. Some write cozy; others write tense thrillers.

Some are debut authors with only one published book; others are multi-published and have had long publishing careers. Some are bestselling authors who may or may not be familiar to you, but being a bestselling author doesn't mean they still don't have to juggle that day job along with their writing. None of the authors featured in this book are named King, Patterson, Roberts, or Evanovich.

So flip through the recipes, find something to whip up for dinner tonight, then while your meal is cooking, sit back and get to know us. Read our bios and our tips. We hope you'll find some new recipes to try, some new authors to read, and some new tips to save time in your busy lives.

If you enjoy *We'd Rather Be Writing: 88 Authors Share Timesaving Dinner Recipes and Other Tips*, please consider posting a review. And if you discover some new favorite authors, please tell your friends about those authors and the books you've enjoyed. Word-of-mouth is an author's best friend, and we count on our readers to provide it.

Bon appétit!
Lois Winston

# Meat Recipes

## Judy Alter's Sloppy Joe

Prep time: 20 min.
Cooking time: 30 min.
Serves 4

1 lb. ground beef
15 oz. canned beans (any variety), rinsed and drained
1/2 cup onion, chopped
1/2 cup celery, diced
2 T. bacon drippings or vegetable oil
1/2 cup ketchup
1-1/2 T. Worcestershire
Dash of Tabasco sauce
1 tsp. salt
1/8 tsp. pepper
1/4 tsp. oregano
1/4 cup dry red wine
1 T. A-1 sauce (optional)

Cook onion in bacon drippings or oil. Add beef and brown. Add remaining ingredients and simmer 20-30 min.

Serve either on buns or in bowls like stew. Leftovers freeze well.

~*~

An award-winning novelist, **Judy Alter** is the author of six Kelly O'Connell Mysteries (*Skeleton in a Dead Space, No Neighborhood for Old Women, Trouble in a Big Box, Danger Comes Home, Deception in Strange Places,* and *Desperate for Death*), three Blue Plate Café Mysteries (*Murder at the Blue Plate Café, Murder at the Tremont House* and *Murder at Peacock Mansion,*) and *The Perfect Coed*, the first book in her Oak Grove Mysteries. Visit Judy at www.judyalter.com.

## Donnell Ann Bell's Taking it Easy—Go Write that Scene—Pot Roast

One of the hardest things to do for a writer on deadline or engrossed in a great scene is to stop and think, what's for dinner? For pot roast lovers and those who want leftovers here's a great, easy recipe that makes family and friends believe you've spent hours in the kitchen.

Prep time: 5 minutes
Cooking time: 3-5 hrs. in oven or 6-8 hrs. in slow cooker
Serves 4-6

3-5 lb. pot roast
1 pkg. Au Jus seasoning
1/2 cup water
1 T. oregano
Crushed garlic, to taste
1 onion, sliced
10 sm. red potatoes, halved
1 bag baby carrots
1 pkg. sliced mushrooms

Center pot roast in baking dish or in a slow cooker. (Note: if using slow cooker, use a liner for faster cleanup.) Sprinkle the packet of Au Jus seasoning on top of the roast. Add water. Surround with potatoes, carrots and mushrooms. Top with oregano and crushed garlic. Spread onion slices throughout.

Cook 3-5 hrs. at 300 degrees or in slow cooker on low 6-8 hrs. Slow cooking creates tender meat and vegetables.

~*~

Bestselling author **Donnell Ann Bell** grew up in the Southwest and today calls Colorado home. A homebody at heart, she concentrates on suspense that might happen in her own neck of the woods, writing "suspense too close to home." Her books have won or been nominated for several prestigious writing awards. Titles include *The Past Came Hunting*, *Deadly Recall*, *Betrayed*, and *Buried Agendas*. Visit Donnell at www.donnellannbell.com.

## Maureen Bonatch's Taco Pizza

Prep time: 5 min.
Cooking time: 20-25 min.
Serves: 4-5

Premade pizza crust
1 lb. ground beef
8 oz. shredded taco cheese blend
1 pkg. Taco seasoning
Shredded lettuce
Salsa
Sour cream
Olives (optional)
Avocado slices (optional)
Refried beans (optional)

Preheat oven to 450 degrees.

Brown ground beef. Drain fat. Add taco seasoning with water as directed on package. Bring to a boil. Reduce heat and simmer uncovered 3-4 min.

Spoon ground beef onto premade pizza crust. Top with cheese. Bake 8-10 min. or until crust is light brown and crisp. Heat optional beans while pizza is cooking.

Cut pizza into 6-8 slices. Top each slice with lettuce, salsa, a dollop of sour cream, and optional olives and/or avocado slices. Serve with optional refried beans.

~*~

Long walks in the beautiful state of Pennsylvania spawned **Maureen Bonatch**'s love of writing. She pens stories boasting laughter, light suspense, and something magical in the hope of sharing her love of finding the extraordinary in the ordinary world. Other interests include fulfilling her role as biker babe to her alpha hubby and surviving (so far) motherhood to twins. Some of her titles include *Destiny Calling* and *Grandma Must Die*. Visit Maureen at www.maureenbonatch.com.

## Ashlyn Chase's Other White Meat with Apples and Leeks

Prep time: 10 min.
Cooking time 30 min.
Serves 6

Nonstick cooking spray or olive oil
2 leeks
3 apples (your choice of variety)
6 boneless pork chops
Garlic salt

Preheat oven to 400 degrees. Lightly coat a large Pyrex pan with cooking spray or olive oil.

Cut leeks into 3" pieces and cut the lower white parts in half. Core and cut the apples into thick slices.

Arrange everything in the pan, covering the bottom completely. Nestle boneless pork chops among the other ingredients, leaving the tops exposed. Sprinkle a little garlic salt over the pork.

Bake 30 min. If desired, brown the pork chops under the broiler a few min.

~*~

Author **Ashlyn Chase** describes herself as an Almond Joy Bar—a little nutty, a little flaky, but basically sweet, and wanting only to give her readers an entertaining treat. Ashlyn writes light paranormal romances. Her works include her Flirting with Fangs series, her Love Spells Gone Wrong series and her upcoming Boston Dragons series. Where there's fire, there's Ash! Visit Ashlyn at www.ashlynchase.com.

## Marni Graff's Beef N Beans

This is an easy one-pot/one-bowl meal all seven of my grandchildren love. You probably have most of the fixings in your pantry. I always double this recipe and freeze half in a foil pan. It keeps for weeks if wrapped sturdily in foil. Can be baked frozen, too, when you need a quick meal—just add 30 min. to the baking time if you don't defrost ahead of time. I serve it with rolls and a salad or blue corn chips and carrot sticks.

Prep time: 20 min.
Cook time: 60 min.
Serves 6

1 lb. ground beef or turkey (or half and half)
1 sm. onion, diced
2 lg. cans baked beans, any flavor
3/4 cup molasses
3/4 cup brown sugar
1 cup salsa
1/2 cup ketchup
3 T. mustard
4 slices bacon, cut into 2" pieces

Preheat oven to 450 degrees.

Brown onions and meat until cooked through. Drain excess fat and place meat and onions in a large mixing bowl.

Add next six ingredients and mix well. Spread in an 11" x 13" casserole dish (or an 8" x 10" deep foil pan for no-wash cleanup!) Dot top with bacon pieces and bake 1 hr. until bacon is crisp.

Leftovers reheat well and can be used a few nights later as the basis for a wrap or hot dog topping.

~*~

Award-winning author **Marni Graff** writes the English Nora Tierney Mysteries and The Trudy Genova Manhattan Mysteries. *The Blue Virgin* and *The Green Remains* won Best British Cozy from Chanticleer Media. *The Scarlet Wench* is on its shortlist. *Death Unscripted* features on-set nurse Trudy Genova, based on Graff's real-life experiences. Visit Marni at www.auntiemwrites.com.

## Elizabeth John's Pork and Sauerkraut

This recipe is great if you have leftover pork loin or plain pork chops. Wrap pork tightly and freeze. When you're ready to use, thaw in the refrigerator. If using fresh pork, brown slightly first and extend cooking time.

Prep time: 5 min.
Cooking time: 30 min.
Serves 6

2 lbs. cooked pork
2 cans or one large bag sauerkraut, rinsed and drained
Small handful of caraway seeds
1 sm. onion, chopped
Olive oil
1/4 cup water
2-3 T. brown sugar
Salt and pepper, to taste

Sauté onion in small amount of olive oil in large pan. While onion is cooking, cut pork into bite sized chunks.

Add sauerkraut, pork, brown sugar, caraway seeds, and water to pan. Stir. Cover and let simmer 15-20 min., checking that there's enough liquid so the dish doesn't burn. Add water or more olive oil to keep moist. Simmer until sauerkraut caramelizes. The longer the pork and sauerkraut cook together, the better. Add salt and pepper to taste.

~*~

**Elizabeth John** writes sweet contemporary romances and romantic suspense novels. Admittedly, she's a TV and movie junkie and has noble intentions to practice yoga daily. Her family and writing life keep her busy. In her spare time, she can be found walking her dogs, sharing a meal with friends, gardening, or relaxing at the beach with her nose in a good book. Her debut novel is *Judging Joey*. Visit Elizabeth at www.elizabethjohn.com.

## Stacy Juba's Easy as Pie Calzone

Prep time: 10 min.
Cooking time: 20-25 min.
Serves 4

Pizza dough
1/4 lb. deli ham
1/4 lb. salami
1/4 lb. American cheese
Egg yolk
Shortening

Preheat oven to 400 degrees.

Rub shortening onto a cookie sheet to keep calzone from sticking.

Roll out dough. Layer one half with ham, salami, and cheese. Fold over and crimp edges with a fork to seal dough closed. Place on cookie sheet.

Make a couple slits in top with fork. Brush egg yolk across top of calzone.

Bake 20-25 min. until golden brown.

~*~

**Stacy Juba** got engaged at Epcot and spent part of her honeymoon at Disneyland Paris. In addition to working on her theme park-set Storybook Valley chick lit series, Stacy has written books about ice hockey, teen psychics, U.S. flag etiquette for kids, and determined women sleuths. Her titles include *Fooling Around With Cinderella, Twenty-Five Years Ago Today, Sink or Swim, Dark Before Dawn, Face-Off,* and *The Flag Keeper.* She is also a freelance editor. Visit Stacy at www.stacyjuba.com.

## Melissa Keir's Hamburg Gravy

Prep time: 5 min.
Cooking time: 20 min.
Serves 4-5

This was a favorite of mine as a child. With five girls and a hungry father, my mom knew how to make budget-friendly meals. Today I like it served over egg noodles or mashed potatoes.

1 lb. ground chuck (more if you want leftovers)
1 med. onion, sliced
3/4 cup milk
Flour
Fresh ground pepper, to taste

Brown ground chuck in a tall-sided frying pan. Drain fat. Add onions and cook until they turn almost clear. Add milk to cover the mixture. Sprinkle in some fresh ground pepper to taste. Turn up heat and cook until just boiling.

Make a paste from a small amount of flour and water. Add to beef mixture to thicken. Serve over egg noodles, mashed potatoes, or rice.

Tip: For a one-dish meal, add some peas to the mixture when you add the milk.

~*~

**Melissa Keir** always wanted to be an author when she wasn't hoping to become a racecar driver. She'd often sneak her mother's books to fantasize about strong alpha males and plucky heroines. Her stories feature small towns and happily-ever-after plots. *The Heartsong Cowboy* and *The Heartbroken Cowboy*, part of the bestselling Cowboy Up boxed sets, have been featured on *USA Today*'s Happily Ever After blog. Visit Melissa at www.melissakeir.com.

## Sandra Master's Nonna's Italian Meatballs

You can feed a large crowd with this recipe, or you can divide into smaller portions, freezing the meatballs and/or sauce to have ready when you need a meal in a hurry. Just defrost in microwave and serve with your favorite pasta.

Prep time: 20 min.
Cooking time: 64 min.
Serves 8-12

2 lbs. chopped beef, at least 80%-20% blend.
3 med. eggs
1/2 – 2/3 cups Parmesan or Parmesan-Reggiano cheese
1/8 cup garlic, chopped (fresh or jarred; if fresh, use slightly less)
1 cup Italian style bread crumbs
Salt and pepper, to taste
1/2 cup milk
Nonstick cooking spray
48 oz. jar spaghetti sauce (any variety)
1 cup dark red wine (any variety)
1/2 tsp. fine sugar
Fresh sprig of basil or oregano (optional)

Preheat oven to 350 degrees. Coat baking sheet with cooking spray.

Mix the chopped beef, eggs, cheese, garlic, salt and pepper in a bowl. Add the crumbs and combine all. Don't overmix. Add milk.

Form meatballs by hand and place on baking sheet. Cook in oven exactly 19 min. Meatballs will be half cooked.

While meatballs are cooking, combine spaghetti sauce, wine, and sugar. Cook to taste, keeping to a low simmer and stirring frequently. Gently place meatballs in sauce and simmer approximately 45 min., adding optional sprig of basil or oregano near end of cooking time. Don't overcook meatballs. They'll become hard.

The above should make about 25 lg. meatballs or more if you make smaller balls. Serving size is 2-3 meatballs per person.

~*~

From a humble beginning in Newark, NJ, a short stay at a convent in Morristown, NJ, to the boardrooms of NYC, to a fantastic career for a broadcasting company in Carlsbad, California, to the rural foothills of the Sierras of Yosemite National Park, **Sandra Masters** has always traveled with pen and notebook. It's been the journey of ten thousand miles. She left her corporate world behind and never looked back. Visit Sandra at www.authorsandramasters.com.

## J.M. Maurer's Slow Cooker Southern Pulled Pork

My sister, who is always on a mission to help those in need, taught me how she makes pulled pork—Southern style. Talk about a timesaver as well as a culinary lifesaver!

I love the simplicity of this recipe. It also adheres to my Less than 5 Ingredients Rule. It cooks while I sleep, freezes well, and makes multiple meals. Plus, the cleanup is simple and quick. If you'd prefer, chicken can be swapped out for the pork.

Prep time: 5 min.
Cooking time: approximately 11-12 hrs.
Serves 12-16

Slow cooker liner
6-8 lbs. pork (I usually get the shoulder)
1 can sweet tea or 1/4 cup water
Splash of oil (approximately 1 T.)

Place liner in slow cooker. With your slow cooker on high, add oil. Allow oil to warm a bit. Place pork in the cooker fat side up. Pour tea or water over meat and cover. Cook on high 30 min. Turn temperature to low and cook 10-12 hrs.

Once the pork is cooked, prepare a workstation next to and in your sink to save cleanup time. Place a plastic bag in your sink. Open the bag and set the edge of your cutting board over one side of the bag so that the bag is open enough that you can easily scrape discarded fat into it.

Remove small portions of meat and place on cutting board. It'll probably fall apart as you take it out. Smile. Your meat is going to be perfectly tender and juicy!

With 2 forks, pull the meat apart, shredding it into strands, scraping fat into the plastic bag. Place pulled pork into storage containers. Ladle juices over meat. Freeze any portions you won't be using. Discard slow cooker liner.

Serve on rolls for pulled sandwiches, over baked sweet potatoes, or on pizza. Other uses include in quesadillas, enchiladas, tacos, burritos, and chili.

~*~

**J.M. Maurer** lives with her family in Chicago. When not saving lives as a registered nurse, she can usually be found scraping at the remnants of a Nutella container, screaming at a hockey game, or putting pen to paper, allowing the "real" crazy voices in her head to come alive. Recent releases include *Seeking Love* and *Seeking Redemption* from her Emerging from Darkness series. Visit J.M. at www.jmmaurer.com.

## Irene Peterson's Last Minute Pork Chops

Boneless pork chops defrost quickly, which makes them perfect for those days when you've forgotten to defrost something for dinner.

Prep time: 10 min.
Cooking time: approximately 30 min.
Serves 4

4 boneless pork chops
Salt and pepper
2 eggs
2 cups Japanese Panko breadcrumbs
Vegetable oil
Duck sauce packets from your last Chinese takeout meal

Place meat in a plastic bag or cover with plastic wrap. Pound meat with a meat tenderizer, hammer, or rolling pin to 3/8" thickness. Too much pounding will make the meat splatter and tear apart.

Once the meat is thinned, remove from plastic. Salt and pepper the meat. Dip in egg wash then breadcrumbs.

Sauté in hot oil until golden on both sides. While pork chops are cooking, heat up a vegetable and Minute Rice or frozen mashed potatoes.

When pork chops are cooked, remove from pan, allow to drain on rack with paper towels underneath to catch any drips.

Serve with duck sauce on the side.

~*~

**Irene Peterson** writes contemporary women's fiction and romance guaranteed to make you laugh. She claims she's a poor example of an author because she only writes when moved to write. However, she's published six books and is working on a seventh. Visit Irene at www.irenepeterson.com.

## Caridad Pineiro's Swiss Chard with Chorizo and Cannellini Beans

If you're juggling work, writing, and family, you want to be able to make a quick dinner that's also healthy and versatile. This dish combines a number of very healthy elements and you can change it up in a variety of ways with whatever you have handy. Plus, you can use it as a side dish or make it a hearty meal by pairing it with some nice crusty bread. I like to fry an egg and put it over the dish to make it a main meal.

Prep time: 10 min.
Cooking time: 20 min.
Serves 2

2 lbs. Swiss chard, chopped
1 cup cured chorizos, chopped
1 sm. onion, chopped
1 clove garlic, chopped
1 T. olive oil
14 oz. can white cannellini beans, drained and rinsed

Heat olive oil in skillet. Add chorizo and cook on medium heat.

While chorizo is cooking, wash Swiss chard, dry, and remove larger tougher stems. Chop.

When chorizo is browned, remove from heat and add onion, garlic and Swiss chard. Wilt the chard and let any juice from the greens evaporate a bit.

Add beans and toss to heat. Add the cooked chorizo to the greens and beans. Salt and pepper to taste. You may want to give it another drizzle of olive oil at the end.

Variations: Instead of the chorizo, try bacon, prosciutto, kielbasa or ham. Instead of the Swiss chard, substitute spinach, mustard greens, kale or escarole.

To bulk up the dish for a heartier meal, cube potatoes or sweet potatoes and cook along with the chorizo. Remove before adding the greens so the cubes will stay crunchy. Add back after you've warmed the beans.

Feeling in a soup kind of mood? Heat chicken broth, place the chorizo, greens and beans in a bowl and add a few ladles of broth to the bowl.

Voila, a dish that can have a myriad of variations! We call dishes like this refrigerator-cleaners in our house, but we also call them something else: Tasty!

~*~

**Caridad Pineiro** is a *New York Times* and *USA Today* bestselling author and Jersey Girl who just wants to write, travel, and spend more time with family and friends. She's the author of over 40 novels/novellas and loves romance novels, super heroes, TV and cooking. Visit Caridad at www.caridad.com.

## Josie Riviera's Chuck Roast BBQ

Prep time: less than 5 min.
Cooking time: 7 hrs.
Serves 4-6

2 lbs. chuck roast
1 packet Italian dressing mix
1 packet Au Jus mix
Rolls

Add roast and contents of packets to slow cooker (Use cooker liner for easy cleanup.) Cook 7 hrs. on high.

When roast is finished cooking, use forks to pull meat apart. Discard fat and gristle.

Serve on rolls. Top off the meal with a side of pasta salad, fruit salad, coleslaw, or tossed salad.

Note: You can cook two roasts and freeze half the pulled meat. Double the Au Jus packet but use only one dressing packet.

~*~

Multi-award winning author **Josie Riviera** writes character-driven novels filled with inspiration and emotion, combining her love of the Romany (Gypsy) lifestyle with historical, Christian, and sweet contemporary romance. Current titles include *Seeking Patience* and *Seeking Catherine* with more to come. Visit Josie at www.josieriviera.wordpress.com.

## C. A. Rowland's Upside-Down Hamburger Pie

Prep time: 15 min.
Cooking time: 40 min.
Serves 6

1 T. olive oil
1/2 lb. ground beef
3/4 cup onions, chopped
3/4 cup celery, chopped
1/4 cup green peppers, chopped
1/2 tsp. salt
1 T. Worcestershire sauce
Dash of pepper
10-1/2 oz. can condensed tomato soup
1 can refrigerated biscuits (containing 8-10 biscuits)

Preheat oven to 450 degrees.

Heat olive oil in frying pan. Add ground beef and brown. Once meat is browned, add onion, celery and green pepper. Cook until vegetables are soft. Add soup, Worcestershire sauce, salt and pepper. Stir and heat through, approximately 5 min.

Pour meat mixture into a 9" round cake pan or square pan. Place individual biscuits on top, side by side, covering meat. The biscuits don't need to cover the meat completely, but you can stretch them to if you prefer.

Bake according to biscuit package directions or until biscuits are golden brown.

Let stand 5 min., then invert baking dish onto a serving platter.

~*~

**C. A. Rowland** writes short stories in multiple genres and is currently finishing her first humorous amateur sleuth mystery novel set in Savannah, Georgia. She's a member of the Virginia Writer's Club, Sisters-In-Crime and the Society of Children's Book Writers and Illustrators. Visit C.A. at www.mostlymystery.com.

## Karen Rose Smith's Creamed Chipped Beef

Creamed chipped beef is a quick comfort food recipe. My mom was an elementary school teacher and evening time was limited. Especially on a cold day, this was a quick and satisfying lunch or supper. After I married and moved away from home, I learned creamed chipped beef is also considered a breakfast food in many parts of the country.

Prep time: 5 min.
Cooking time: 15-20 min.
Serves 6

4 T. butter
1/2 lb. chipped dried beef
3 T. flour
2-1/2 cups milk
1/8 tsp. pepper
6 slices bread, toasted or baked potatoes

Melt butter in 12" frying pan with high sides.

Tear chipped beef into the butter and brown approximately 4 min. on medium heat. Stir in flour, continuing to stir until all absorbed. Turn burner to medium-high and slowly pour in milk. Stir until thickened. Stir in pepper. Pour over toast or potatoes.

~*~

*USA Today* bestselling author **Karen Rose Smith** will have her 90th novel published in 2016. She writes the Caprice De Luca Home Staging Mystery series and the Search For Love series. Families are a strong theme in her novels. Her passions include caring for her four rescued cats, gardening, cooking and photography. Visit Karen at www.karenrosesmith.com.

## Aubrey Wynne's Golden Pork Chops

Prep time: 10-15 min.
Cooking time: 45-55 min.
Serves 4-6

Nonstick cooking spray
4-6 pork chops, any cut
1 can golden mushroom soup
Petite potatoes (or 4 quartered large ones)
Fresh mushrooms (optional)
Small bag baby carrots (may substitute with squash, zucchini or other vegetables)
Garlic powder
1/4 cup finely chopped shallots (optional)
Fresh sprigs rosemary (or dried flakes)
Fresh sprigs thyme (or dried flakes)
Pepper, to taste

Preheat oven to 350 degrees. Lightly spray 9" x 13" baking pan or shallow casserole dish.

Place pork chops in bottom of baking pan or dish. Add mushrooms over pork chops. Spread soup over the pork chops/mushrooms. Place potatoes and carrots around meat. Sprinkle shallots, garlic and pepper over entire dish. Place the sprigs of rosemary and thyme on top or lightly sprinkle with dried flakes.

Bake 45-55 min. or until carrots and potatoes are easily poked with a fork. (If thinly sliced, 35-45 min.)

~*~

**Aubrey Wynne** resides in the Midwest with her husband, dogs, horses, mule and barn cats. Elementary teacher by trade, champion of children and animals by conscience, and author by night, her obsessions include history, travel, trail riding and all things Christmas. Her award-winning stories include *Merry Christmas, Henry*, *Pete's Mighty Purty Privies* and her latest release, *Dante's Gift,* a mix of contemporary and vintage holiday romance. Visit Aubrey at www.aubreywynneauthor.com.

# Pasta Recipes

## Krista Ames' Pasta Salad

Prep time: 20 min.
Cooking time: 10 min.
Serves 5

1 box spaghetti
1 bottle Italian Dressing
1 can black olives, drained
1 pt. cherry tomatoes, sliced
1 can chunk crabmeat (optional)

Bring large pot of water to boil. Cook spaghetti according to package directions, approximately 10 min. Drain.

In large bowl, mix pasta with half a bottle Italian dressing. Add black olives, cherry tomatoes and optional crabmeat.

Refrigerate until chilled. After chilling, pasta will have soaked up much of the dressing. At this point add as much of the rest of the bottle as you choose.

~*~

Romance author **Krista Ames** is a full-time author, mom, and wife who resides in northern lower Michigan with her husband and four children. Her latest book is *Second Nature*. Visit Krista at www.kristaames.com

## Maya Corrigan's Mediterranean Pasta with Artichokes, Olives, and Tomatoes

For a non-vegetarian version of this recipe, add 1 lb. peeled, deveined shrimp.

Prep time: 10 min.
Cook time: 15 min.
Serves 4

1/2 – 3/4 lb. linguine or penne pasta
4 cloves garlic, chopped
2 T. olive oil
14-15 oz. canned chickpeas (optional)
14-15 oz. canned whole artichoke hearts, cut in quarters
14-15 oz. canned diced tomatoes
1/4 cup diced sun dried tomatoes in oil
1/4 cup Kalamata olives
2-3 oz. crumbled feta cheese

Cook the linguine or penne according to package directions while making the sauce.

Heat oil in a 12" skillet over medium heat until hot but not smoking. Sauté garlic in oil no more than 1 min. Don't let it turn brown.

If using shrimp, add them to the pan and cook until opaque on outside, approximately 1 min. Remove shrimp from skillet and set aside.

Pour tomatoes with juice into skillet. Bring to a boil. Add artichoke hearts, dried tomatoes, and optional chickpeas. Continue cooking until ingredients are hot.

Add shrimp back in and cook until they're done. Cooking time varies by size of shrimp. They should be C-shaped, rather than curled tightly into an O, a sign that they're overdone.

Drain the pasta, add to skillet, and mix with the sauce. Stir in olives.

Sprinkle with crumbled feta just before serving.

~*~

Award-winning mystery author **Maya Corrigan** combines food and murder in her Five-Ingredient Mystery series set in a Chesapeake Bay town. Titles include *By Cook or By Crook*, *Scam Chowder*, and the upcoming *Final Fondue*. Before taking up a life of crime (on the page,) she taught college courses on writing, drama, and detective fiction. Visit Maya at www.mayacorrigan.com.

## Helena Fairfax's Vegetarian Pasta with Leeks, Zucchini and Parmesan

This is the quickest recipe I know, but although it's so simple, it's also tasty and healthy and perfect for vegetarians. In the UK we call zucchini "courgettes." They're the same vegetable, but I think we harvest our courgettes when they're smaller. A small zucchini would be best for this recipe.

Prep time: 10 min.
Cooking time: approximately 20 min.
Serves 2-3

Spaghetti (enough for 2-3 people)
Olive oil
1 leek, chopped
2 cloves garlic, chopped finely
1 sm. zucchini, sliced
1 green pepper, seeded and chopped (optional)
1 cup white wine
Salt and pepper
Parmesan cheese, grated

Cook spaghetti according to package directions while preparing vegetables.

Heat olive oil in a pan over moderate heat. Add leek, garlic, zucchini, and optional green pepper. Keep stirring vegetables. When zucchini has softened and darkened in color, add the white wine. Bring to a boil to reduce the liquid slightly. Season with salt and pepper.

When the spaghetti is cooked, drain the water and toss spaghetti in with the cooked vegetables. Sprinkle with grated Parmesan cheese before serving.

~*~

English author **Helena Fairfax** lives in an old Victorian mill town in Yorkshire, near the home of the Brontë sisters. Her contemporary romances feature swoon-worthy heroines and heroes. Helena's novels have been shortlisted for several awards, including a New Writers' Scheme Award, the Global E-Book Awards, the Exeter Novel Prize, and her favorite—"The Most Romantic Love Scene Ever." *Palace of Deception* is her latest release. Visit Helena at www.helenafairfax.com.

## Shelley Freydont's Pesto Pasta

I make fresh pesto in summer and freeze leftovers for winter.

Prep time: 10 min.
Cooking time: 10 min.
Serves 4

One large bunch fresh basil
4-6 cloves garlic, to taste
Salt
Olive oil
Pignoli nuts (optional)
Parmesan or Romano cheese, freshly grated
1 box pasta (any variety but angel hair or rotini gives you more pesto per pasta)

Boil water in a large pot. Add small amount of salt and olive oil. Cook pasta al dente. Drain.

While pasta is cooking, strip leaves and smaller stems from central basil stems. Rinse and leave in colander.

Cut garlic in half and place in blender or food processor. Chop small. Add basil and oil, stuffing the leaves toward the bottom. Add optional pine nuts. Blend until everything is chopped fine, continue to add oil until smooth.

Place warm pasta in a large bowl, stir in pesto. Toss until pasta is coated. Any leftovers can be refrigerated or frozen.

Cheese can be added to the pasta or served separately to each person's taste. Salt and pepper to individual taste.

Options: Mix cubed broiled, sautéed, or roasted chicken with the pesto pasta or add halved heirloom cherry tomatoes.

Serve with Caprese or green salad and loaf of crusty bread.

~*~

*New York Times* bestselling author **Shelley Freydont/Shelley Noble** writes the Liv Montgomery Celebration Bay Mysteries and the Newport Gilded Age Mysteries, beginning with *A Gilded Grave*. She's also written the Kate MacDonald Sudoku Mysteries and the Lindy Haggerty Dance Company Mysteries. As Shelley Noble, she writes women's fiction, most recently, *Whisper Beach*. A former professional dancer and choreographer, Shelley lives at the Jersey shore and loves puzzles, lighthouses and antique carousels. Visit Shelley at www.shelleyfreydont.com and www.shelleynoble.com.

## Rosie Genova's Hot Pasta with Cold Tomato Sauce (inspired by Father Tom)

This recipe makes more than enough "sauce" for a pound of pasta. It's also good the next day as a cold pasta salad—add olives, cubed cheese, and chickpeas for a different take on the dish.

Prep time: 10 min. (plus at least 3 hrs. to marinate)
Cooking time: 12-15 min.
Serves 4

Approximately 10 fresh plum tomatoes, chopped well
5 oz. pkg. fresh arugula or other hardy baby green, chopped well
3/4 – 1 cup olive oil
1-2 cloves garlic, chopped well
Sea salt and freshly grated pepper, to taste
1 box gemelli pasta (or other variety)
Grated Romano cheese

Mix together chopped tomatoes, arugula, and garlic. At this stage, I season with two generous teaspoons of sea salt and several twists of the pepper grinder. Before serving, taste and adjust seasonings to preference.

Pour olive oil over mixture. Let mixture marinate at least 3 hrs., taking care to stir several times. The arugula will soften and sweeten in the oil and juices from the tomatoes.

Shortly before serving, boil water and cook pasta according to package directions. Drain and divide onto four plates. Add sauce. Sprinkle with grated Romano cheese.

~*~

A Jersey girl born and bred, national bestselling author **Rosie Genova** left her heart at the shore, which serves as the setting for her Italian

Kitchen Mysteries, a series of cozy mysteries with romantic interruptions. Titles to date include *Murder in Marinara*, *The Wedding Soup Murder*, and her latest release, *A Dish Best Served Cold*. Her books have been finalists for several prestigious awards. Visit Rosie at www.rosiegenova.com.

## Tara Neale's Tempting Dynamic Dinner Duo

A decade ago as a single mom with four growing teens, a full-time job, and a passion for my writing that was at the time only a hobby, dinnertime was always a challenge. After a long day at a stressful job, the last thing I wanted to do was come home to cook. Dinners that were nutritious, cheap, and that the kids could throw in the oven themselves if Mommy was running late were the way to go. So I often spent my Sunday afternoons making up several casseroles that would get us most of the way through the week. My lasagna and cannelloni were always favorites.

The best thing about this combo is that the extra cheese mixture that you make for the lasagna becomes a second meal for the week.

### Cheese Mixture for both Lasagna and Cannelloni

Prep time: 5 min.

2 cups cottage cheese (plain or low-fat)
1-1/2 cups ricotta
1 cup mascarpone cheese
1/2 cup grated Parmesan cheese
1 tsp. dried Italian spices (or chopped fresh basil and oregano)
Pepper, to taste

Mix all ingredients together.

### Lasagna

Prep time: 20 min.
Cooking time: 40-45 min.
Serves 6

Cheese mixture (recipe above)

1 can tomatoes
1 jar spaghetti sauce
1 pkg. lasagna noodles
1 lb. hamburger, cooked and drained (or 2 cups of sautéed veggie mixture of zucchini, eggplant, onion, garlic and mushrooms)
2 cups shredded mozzarella cheese

Preheat oven to 300 degrees.

Pour half the can of tomatoes on the bottom of glass casserole dish, then layer with uncooked lasagna noodles to cover the bottom of the dish.

Spread one-third of spaghetti sauce, 1/2 cup of cheese mixture and half the meat or veggies over noodles. Repeat. Top layer should only be noodles, spaghetti sauce, and remaining canned tomatoes.

Cover in foil and refrigerate until needed (up to 2 or 3 days.)

Bake covered 30 min. Remove foil, sprinkle with mozzarella and bake an additional 10-15 min. until cheese is melted, bubbling and slightly brown.

## Cannelloni

Prep time: 20 min.
Cooking time: 25 min.
Serves 6

Remaining cheese mixture
1 pkg. cannelloni noodles
1 lg. egg
1 cup frozen spinach, thawed and drained
1 jar spaghetti or cheese sauce
2 cups mozzarella cheese

In boiling salted water, pre-cook cannelloni noodles and drain. Allow to cool.

Preheat oven to 300 degrees.

Mix egg and spinach into remaining cheese sauce. Spread half the spaghetti or cheese sauce in the bottom of a casserole dish. Using either a small spoon or icing pipette, fill noodles with cheese mixture. Arrange stuffed noodles in dish. Cover with remaining sauce and cheese. Store in refrigerator until ready to cook.

Bake covered 15-20 min. Remove foil and allow cheese to brown for another 5 min.

Two dinners ready in less than half an hour and if you have a large family, buying in bulk makes things cheaper, too.

~*~

Romance and romantic suspense author **Tara Neale** is a home-schooling mom and indie author. When not writing, her days are filled rushing around London after her delightful special needs daughter as they explore and learn together. Her books include *The Arrangement*, *My Country 'Tis of Thee*, *Labor's End*, and *Shared Burdens*. Visit Tara at www.taraneale.com.

## Alice Orr's Pasta à la Capri

Prep time: 20 min.
Cooking time: 30 min.
Serves 4

Nonstick cooking spray
1 box penne pasta
1-1/2 cups red pasta sauce
1/2 cup half and half
1/2 cup grated fresh Parmesan cheese, plus more for top
1/8 tsp. allspice
Small amount cayenne pepper
Small amount hand-zested lemon peel
Salt and pepper, to taste
1 pint grape tomatoes, halved lengthwise
8 oz. mozzarella, cubed small
2 tsp. dried basil
1 tsp. dried parsley
Small amount butter or butter substitute
Seasoned breadcrumbs
Paprika

Preheat oven to 375 degrees. Coat 13" x 9" baking dish with cooking spray.

Cook pasta according to package directions, no longer than al dente.

Heat sauce in a skillet over low heat. Stir in half and half. Add Parmesan, allspice, lemon zest, salt and pepper. Simmer a few minutes until Parmesan melts and sauce is smooth. Stir in grape tomatoes, mozzarella, basil and parsley.

Fold cream sauce into cooked pasta. Pour into baking dish. Top with dots of butter. Sprinkle with breadcrumbs, additional Parmesan and paprika.

Bake approximately 30 min. or until cheese is melted.

Serve with green salad and crusty bread.

~*~

**Alice Orr** is the author of thirteen novels, two novellas, a memoir, and *No More Rejections: 50 Secrets to Writing a Manuscript that Sells*. She's a former book editor and literary agent, now living her dream as a full-time writer of romantic suspense stories. Current titles include *A Wrong Way Home* and *A Year of Summer Shadows*, both part of her Riverton Road Romantic Suspense series. Visit Alice at www.aliceorrbooks.com.

## Laurel Peterson's Pasta with Butternut Squash Sauce

Prep time: 10 min.
Cooking time: approximately 20 min.
Serves 4 or more, depending on size of squash

1 med. butternut squash, peeled, seeded, and cut into thin slices
2 oz. butter or 1-2 T. olive oil
1 leek, chopped
1 stalk celery, chopped
1/2 – 1 cup chicken stock, depending on size of the squash
Salt and pepper
Grated nutmeg (freshly grated is best)
2/3 cup heavy cream (optional)
Freshly grated Parmesan cheese
1 box pasta (sturdier pastas such as ziti and fettuccini work best)

Melt half the butter in a large pot. Add leek, celery, and squash slices, stirring to coat with butter. Add small amount of stock and cover. (Add enough so the squash doesn't burn, but not too much so that the sauce will be runny.)

Cook approximately 20 min., adding more stock from time to time, if necessary, to keep moist. When squash is soft, add salt, pepper and nutmeg to taste.

Process the sauce until smooth with an immersion blender or in a blender or food processor. Return to pan to keep warm.

Cook pasta. Add cream to sauce. Drain pasta. Add sauce and remainder of butter. Serve with Parmesan cheese on the side or add in when you mix in the sauce.

~*~

**Laurel Peterson** is an English professor whose debut mystery *Shadow Notes* will be available in March 2016. She has also had poetry published in many small literary magazines and has two poetry chapbooks, *That's the Way the Music Sounds* and *Talking to the Mirror*. She also co-edited a collection of essays on women's justice titled *(Re)Interpretations: The Shapes of Justice in Women's Experience*. Visit Laurel at www.laurelpeterson.com.

# Renée Reynolds' Creamy Spinach Tortellini with Tomato Sauce

Prep time: 5 min.
Cooking time: 15-20 min.
Serves 6

16 oz. pkg. frozen cheese tortellini pasta
1-1/2 cups heavy cream
2 T. all-purpose flour
2 T. extra virgin olive oil
1 sm. onion, chopped
3 cloves garlic, minced or crushed
14.5 oz. can diced tomatoes, undrained
3 cups fresh or 10 oz. pkg. chopped frozen spinach, thawed
1/2 tsp. basil
1/2 tsp. oregano
1/2 tsp. ground black pepper
1/2 cup Parmesan cheese, grated, plus extra for garnish

Cook tortellini according to package directions. Drain well.

In a small bowl, whisk together heavy cream and flour.

In a large, deep skillet, heat olive oil over medium-high heat. Add garlic and onion. Cook until translucent, stirring often, about 2 min.

Add spinach, stirring frequently until spinach begins to wilt, about 2 min. If using thawed frozen spinach, squeeze dry before adding to skillet, stirring until heated through.

Mix in undrained tomatoes and spices. Gradually whisk or stir in heavy cream mixture and cook, stirring constantly, until mixture thickens, about 4 min.

Add tortellini and gently stir to combine and reheat the pasta. Serve immediately. Sprinkle with extra grated Parmesan, to taste.

Want to make this even easier? Cook a 16 oz. pkg. of cheese tortellini according to package directions and drain well. In the pot used to boil the pasta, pour in a 15 oz. jar of garlic Alfredo sauce and 12 oz. jar tomato and basil sauce. Add 10 oz. thawed, drained, and chopped spinach. Stir ingredients frequently over medium-high heat until just boiling, about 5 min. Add pasta and stir until heated through. Serve immediately. Sprinkle with grated Parmesan cheese, as desired.

**Renée Reynolds** pens smart, sassy, and seductive happily-ever-afters of the historical variety, with titles like *Lord Love a Duke, A Marquis For All Seasons,* and *Earl Crazy*. She's a city girl living the country life in Texas with the hubs, kiddos, and a menagerie of pets. Visit Renée at www.obstinateheadstronggirl.wordpress.com.

## Judy Penz Sheluk's Easy Peasy Veggie Lasagna

Prep time: 15 min.
Cooking time: 70 min.
Serves 4-6

Nonstick cooking spray
3-1/2 cups pasta sauce
6 lasagna noodles, uncooked
15 oz. ricotta cheese
1 cup shredded mozzarella cheese (you can also use cheddar or 1/2 cup each mozzarella and cheddar)
2 cups chopped raw vegetables (any variety)

Preheat oven to 375. Coat 11" x 7" baking dish with cooking spray.

Spread 1/4 of the sauce on bottom of baking dish. Arrange 3 lasagna noodles on top of sauce. Top noodles with 1/4 cup of sauce, all the ricotta cheese, half the shredded cheese, and all the vegetables. Arrange remaining noodles on top, cover with remaining sauce.

Cover with aluminum foil and bake until mixture is sizzling hot and noodles are tender, approximately 1 hr. Remove foil, sprinkle with remaining shredded cheese and bake uncovered 5 min. Let stand 5 min. before cutting.

~*~

**Judy Penz Sheluk** is the author of the debut mystery, *The Hanged Man's Noose*. Her short crime fiction is included in *The Whole She-Bang 2* and *World Enough and Crime*. In her less mysterious pursuits, Judy works as a freelance writer/editor. She is currently Editor of Home BUILDER Magazine and Senior Editor, New England Antiques Journal. Visit Judy at www.judypenzsheluk.com.

## Lois Winston's Mushroom Pasta

I love Portobello mushrooms. They're a perfect meat substitute when you want something other than meatballs or sausage with your pasta. Trust me, you won't miss the meat!

Prep time: 5 min.
Cooking time: 20 min.
Serves 4

1 box whole-grain spaghetti
1-1/2 T. olive oil
1 med. onion, chopped
2 cloves garlic, chopped
1/2 cup white wine
4 cups Portobello mushrooms, chopped
3 T. fresh parsley, chopped
2 T. lemon juice
4 cups fresh baby spinach
Freshly grated Parmesan cheese

Cook spaghetti according to package directions. Drain. Rinse. Toss with a tsp. of olive oil and set aside.

While spaghetti is cooking, heat remaining olive oil in a large skillet. Cook the onions and garlic until the onions are soft. Add the wine and cook approximately 5 min. until most of the wine has evaporated. Add the mushrooms and sauté 6-7 min.

Add parsley, lemon juice, and spinach. Sauté 1 min. until spinach wilts. Add pasta. Heat through.

Sprinkle with fresh Parmesan cheese after plating.

~*~

*USA Today* bestselling and award-winning author **Lois Winston** writes mystery, romance, romantic suspense, chick lit, women's fiction, children's chapter books, and nonfiction under her own name and her Emma Carlyle pen name. *Kirkus Reviews* dubbed her critically acclaimed Anastasia Pollack Crafting Mystery series, "North Jersey's more mature answer to Stephanie Plum." Visit Lois at www.loiswinston.com.

# *Poultry Recipes*

## Rose Anderson's Slow Cooker Chicken with Mushrooms

Prep time: 20 min.
Cooking time: 4 hrs.
Serves 4

1-1/2 lbs. chicken breast, cut into chunks or use whole chicken tenders
1 lb. mushrooms (any variety), sliced
1 lg. onion, chopped
1 clove garlic, minced
1 cup table wine (any variety)
1 cup water or milk
16 oz. Neufchatel cream cheese, cut into cubes
1/2 stick butter, cut into cubes (May substitute any mild-flavored oil)
1 cup grated Parmesan cheese (plus additional cheese at the table)
Salt and fresh cracked black pepper, to taste

Note: Directions are given for using a slow cooker. You can also make this dish by cooking over medium heat in a covered skillet, stirring frequently, or bake in a covered casserole at 350 degrees for 1 hr.

Melt butter in skillet. Sear chicken on all sides until brown. No need to cook through at this point. Add browned chicken to slow cooker. Partially cook onion and garlic in the same skillet, then add to slow cooker.

Deglaze pan with wine and scrape up any browned bits. Set aside.

Add sliced mushrooms and cream cheese to slow cooker. Stir in wine from deglazed pan, water or milk, and Parmesan cheese. Cook 4 hrs. or until chicken is cooked through.

~*~

**Rose Anderson** is a multi-published award-winning author and dilettante who loves great conversation and delights in interesting things to weave into her stories. Rose also writes across genres under her

Madeline Archer pen name. She lives with her family and small menagerie amid oak groves and prairie in the rolling glacial hills of the upper Midwest. Visit Rose at www.calliopeswritingtablet.com.

## Judy Baker's Chicken Skillet

Prep time: 10 min.
Cooking time: 20 min.
Serves 6

1/2 lb. linguine
6 sm. boneless, skinless chicken breast halves
1/2 tsp. black pepper
2 T. olive oil
6 sm. yellow squash or zucchini (or 3 of each), cubed
4 cloves garlic, minced
1-1/2 cups shredded Italian 3-cheese blend
1/4 cup chopped fresh basil
1/4 cup grated Parmesan cheese

Cook linguine according to package directions.

While linguine is cooking, sprinkle chicken with pepper. Heat 1 T. oil in large nonstick skillet on medium heat. Cook chicken 5-7 min. on each side or until thoroughly cooked.

Add squash and stir-fry 3 min. Add garlic and cook another 3 min. or until squash is tender.

Drain pasta, reserving 1/4 cup cooking water. Toss pasta with the reserved water, then place on platter. Top with chicken and squash, then basil and cheese.

~*~

**Judy Baker** writes historical western romances, but her alter ego Anna Sugg writes contemporary romance and romantic suspense. Although she lives in Utah and loves being surrounded by mountains and desert valleys, she's a southerner at heart. She enjoys RVing, stargazing, digging in her wildflower garden, science fiction, coffee, sweet southern tea, and the ocean. Visit Judy at www.judybaker.coffeecup.com.

## Paula Gail Benson's Cheesy Turkey Slow Cooker Meatloaf

Prep time: 20 min.
Cooking time: 5-7 hrs.
Serves 4-6

1-1/2 – 2 lbs. ground white meat turkey
1 cup crushed Cheez-It crackers
1 egg
1/2 cup ketchup
2 lg. baking potatoes, sliced
2 lg. carrots, sliced
Sm. onion, sliced
1 red, green, or yellow pepper (or combination,) cut in strips
Nonstick cooking spray or slow cooker liner
1/2 cup water

Place the crackers in a zip-top plastic bag and crush with rolling pin into meal consistency.

Mix the ground turkey, egg, and cracker crumbs together. Mold into a loaf.

Coat bottom and sides of slow cooker with cooking spray or use liner for faster cleanup. Place potatoes, carrots, and onion in bottom of slow cooker. Place meatloaf on top of vegetables. Surround with pepper strips. Spread ketchup evenly on top of meatloaf. Pour water around edges of the cooker over the vegetables. Cover and cook on low 5-7 hr.

Leftovers can be served cold the next day as sandwiches with mayonnaise, cheddar cheese, bread and butter pickles, and your choice of bread.

~*~

Legislative attorney and former law librarian, **Paula Gail Benson**'s short stories have appeared online and in *Mystery Times Ten 2013*; *A Tall*

*Ship, a Star, and Plunder*; *A Shaker of Margaritas: That Mysterious Woman*, and *Fish or Cut Bait: a Guppy Anthology*. She blogs at Little Sources of Joy, the Stiletto Gang, and Writers Who Kill. Visit Paula at www.paulagailbenson.com.

# Kris Bock's Quick Enchilada Casserole

This recipe is not exactly traditional, but it's my quicker and healthier version of an enchilada casserole. To reduce the time it takes to assemble the dish, I use tortilla chips instead of corn tortillas that must be toasted first.

Prep time: 30 min.
Cooking time: 45 min.
Serves 8 (for smaller families leftovers can be reheated the next day)

Nonstick cooking spray
Several handfuls of tortilla chips
1 lg. onion, chopped
1 T. cooking oil
3 cups cooked chicken, chopped
10 oz. can cream of chicken soup
12-15 oz. jar red enchilada sauce
15 oz. canned pinto beans, drained and rinsed
Red chili powder, to taste (optional)
1-2 cups shredded cheddar, Monterey Jack, or Mexican blend cheese

Preheat oven to 350 degrees.

Lightly spray 9" x 13" casserole dish. Scatter broken tortilla chips in bottom of dish. (This is a great way to use the broken chips at the bottom of the bag. It doesn't really matter what size they are or if they're stale.)

Sauté onion in oil until golden. Add chicken. You can also use fresh chicken but make sure you heat it long enough to cook through. Add cream of chicken soup, enchilada sauce, pinto beans, and red chili powder. Mix well.

Pour the chicken and sauce mixture over the tortilla chips. Cover with another layer of broken tortilla chips. Top with a layer of shredded cheese.

Bake approximately 45 min.

Options: Try black beans instead of pinto beans, or sautéed ground beef or turkey instead of chicken.

Skip the meat and add extra vegetables such as bell peppers, corn, zucchini, summer squash, or mushrooms, or use a bag of frozen mixed vegetables to save chopping time.

Try using green enchilada sauce. Use chopped green chili instead of the red chili powder. Check the Mexican section of your grocery store for canned green chilies and both kinds of enchilada sauce.

~*~

Romantic suspense author **Kris Bock** writes novels featuring outdoor adventures and Southwestern landscapes. In *Counterfeits*, stolen Rembrandt paintings bring danger to a small New Mexico town. *Whispers in the Dark* features archaeology and intrigue among ancient Southwest ruins. In *What We Found*, a young woman finds a murder victim in the woods. *The Mad Monk's Treasure* and *The Dead Man's Treasure* involve New Mexico treasure hunts. Visit Kris at www.krisbock.com.

## Ava Bradley's Timesaving Enchiladas

Prep time: 15 min.
Cooking time: 20 min.
Serves 4

4 corn or flour tortillas
1 cooked chicken breast, cubed or fork-shredded
1 cup grated Jack cheese
1 cup grated cheddar cheese
2 cups enchilada sauce (your choice)
Sour cream
Avocado
Corn chips

Preheat oven to 325 degrees.

Spread a small amount of enchilada sauce on the inside of the tortillas. Spread chicken on top of sauce. Add some cheese. Roll up tortilla.

Spread a small amount of enchilada sauce on the bottom of a ceramic baking dish. Place enchiladas in dish. Cover with enchilada sauce and sprinkle the remaining cheese on top.

Bake 20-40 min.

Top with sour cream and serve with avocado slices and corn chips.

One each is more than enough for a dinner meal, so if you're cooking for two, you have a second meal. I like green sauce and my husband likes red, so we use both and cook them in the same dish. Twenty minutes is usually enough time to heat through and melt all the cheese. Forty minutes will produce extra-brown and crunchy enchiladas.

~*~

**Ava Bradley** put her fascination with doomsday prepping into *Kiss Me*

*Before Dawn*, a dystopian romance about a futuristic bounty hunter who hates vampires, and the vampire she's forced to work with on her toughest case yet. Visit Ava at www.avabradley.com.

## Judy Copek's Chicken Little

Prep time: 5 min.
Cooking time: 1 hr.
Serves 4

1 stick butter
1 cup uncooked rice (any variety)
1 med. onion, chopped
27 oz. chicken broth
2 lbs. (approximately) chicken pieces
Rosemary or thyme (optional)

Preheat oven to 350 degrees.

Cut chicken into smallish pieces (halve breasts, etc.)

Melt butter. Pour into a 9" x 13" glass casserole.

Add rice, onion and broth. Place chicken pieces on rice mixture. Sprinkle with rosemary or thyme.

Bake uncovered 1 hr.

~*~

**Judith Copek** was an information systems nerd for twenty-plus years who likes to show technology's humor and quirkiness along with its scary aspects in her books. Her novels include *Festival Madness, World of Mirrors* and *The Shadow Warriors*. *Festival Madness* is set in and around Boston and at the Burning Man Festival. The other two take place in Germany. Judith has also published poems, short stories and a memoir. Visit Judy at www.judycopek.com.

## Melinda Curtis' Slow Cooker Shredded Buffalo Chicken

Prep time: 5 min.
Cooking time: 5-7 hrs.
Serves 6

Nonstick cooking spray or slow cooker liner
6 uncooked chicken breasts
1/2 cup BBQ sauce
1/4 cup yellow mustard
1/4 cup apple cider vinegar

Spray your slow cooker with cooking spray, or for quicker cleanup use a liner.

Place chicken in slow cooker and top with BBQ sauce, yellow mustard, and vinegar. Cover and cook on high 5 hrs. or on low 7 hrs.

When 30 min. of cooking time is left, shred the chicken and stir well. Replace cover and continue cooking.

Serve over lettuce or on bread or rolls (any variety.)

~*~

Award winning, *USA Today* bestseller **Melinda Curtis** writes the Harmony Valley series of sweet and emotional romances and the sweet romantic comedy Bridesmaid series. Brenda Novak said, "*Season of Change* has found a place on my keeper shelf." Melinda also writes independently published, hotter romances as Mel Curtis. Jayne Ann Krentz called *Blue Rules* a "Sharp, sassy, modern version of a screwball comedy from Hollywood's Golden Age except a lot hotter." Visit Melinda at www.melindacurtis.net.

## Nancy Eady's Chicken Casserole

This casserole can be made in advance and frozen before being baked. Allow casserole to thaw in the refrigerator 24 hrs., then bake as directed. For smaller families, halve the recipe or divide into two smaller casserole dishes and freeze one. The smaller casserole will still need to bake 25-30 min.

Prep time: 10 min.
Cooking time: 25-30 min.
Serves 6-8

Nonstick cooking spray
6-8 pre-cooked chicken breasts, cut into bite-size pieces
2 cans cream of chicken soup
1 cup sour cream
1 roll Ritz crackers
1 stick margarine
2 T. poppy seeds (optional)

Preheat oven to 350 degrees.

Spray casserole large enough to hold ingredients. Place chicken in bottom of casserole.

In a separate bowl, mix together cream of chicken soup and sour cream. Pour over chicken.

Place crackers in a zip-top plastic bag and crush into crumbs with rolling pin. Sprinkle crumbs over soup.

Slice margarine into pats and dot top of cracker crumbs. Sprinkle optional poppy seeds over top of casserole.

Bake 25-30 min. until the casserole bubbles. Serve immediately.

~*~

**Nancy Eady** is a writer living in central Alabama. She's the author of the blog *Tales from the Mom-Side: My Adventures as a Working Mom* and is currently developing The Webster County Mystery series. Visit Nancy at www.workingmomadventures.com.

## Kit Frazier's 15-Minute Texas Quesadillas with Chicken Fajita Seasoning

Prep time: 5 min.
Cooking time: 8-15 min.
Serves 6-8

1 T. chili powder
Cumin, to taste
1 tsp. paprika
1/4 tsp. roasted cayenne pepper
1/4 tsp. garlic powder
1 tsp. salt
1 tsp. ground black pepper
2 T. olive oil
2 lbs. skinless chicken breasts
Salt and pepper, to taste
Chicken fajita seasoning, to taste
12 tri-colored baby peppers, seeded and sliced into strips
1 sm. onion, sliced
1 stick butter
12 lg. flour tortillas
2-1/2 cups grated queso blanco or Monterey Jack cheese
Pico de gallo
Guacamole
Sour cream
Sliced jalapenos
Limes

For seasoning, whisk together first seven ingredients in small bowl. Set aside. (Note: You can double the recipe and freeze half in an airtight container to use for another meal.)

Season chicken with salt, pepper, and fajita seasoning. Heat 1 T. olive oil in skillet over high heat. Sear chicken on almost-high heat until done. Remove from the skillet and shred. Set aside.

Add remaining olive oil to skillet over high heat. Sear peppers and onions until peppers have a few dark brown/black areas, 3-4 min. Remove and set aside, reserving half to serve with quesadillas.

Sizzle 1/2 T. butter in a separate skillet over medium heat. Place a flour tortilla in skillet. Sprinkle tortilla with half a handful of grated cheese, then sprinkle shredded chicken on top. Add cooked peppers and onions. Top with a little more grated cheese and a second tortilla.

When tortilla is toasty-golden on bottom, carefully flip the quesadilla, adding another 1/2 T. butter to the skillet to prevent sticking. Cook until second side is golden. Repeat with the remaining tortillas and fillings.

Cut each quesadilla into wedges and plate it with pico de gallo, sour cream, guacamole, sliced jalapenos, sliced lime wedges and extra pepper and onion sauté.

~*~

**Kit Frazier** is an award-winning mystery author whose books have been Mystery Guild Book-of-the-Month selections and who's been named Author of the Month at Barnes & Noble. Titles include *Scoop* and *Dead Copy*, among others. A former journalist, Kit lives on a working cattle ranch outside of Austin, Texas. Visit Kit at www.kitfrazier.com.

## Linda Gordon Hengerer's Chicken and Noodles

Prep time: 10 min.
Cook time: 15 min.
Serves 4

1 lb. chicken breasts or pre-cut chicken strips
8 oz. pkg. egg noodles
2 T. all-purpose flour
1 tsp. Everglades seasoning (or just use salt and pepper)
8 oz. mushrooms, sliced
1 sweet onion, diced
1 cup chicken stock
2 T. olive oil, divided
2 T. butter, divided
Salt and pepper
Fresh or dried herbs (optional)

Heat water for egg noodles. Cook noodles in salted water according to package directions.

In a large zip-top plastic bag, place flour, seasoning, salt (if not in seasoning,) and pepper. Mix to combine. Add chicken. Toss to coat chicken.

In large sauté pan, heat 1 T. oil on medium heat until shimmering. Add chicken in one layer. Brown on both sides. Remove from pan.

Add remaining oil and 1 T. butter to pan. Once butter is melted, add mushrooms and onions. Season to taste with salt and pepper. Cook until softened, about 5 min. Add chicken, chicken stock (more or less, depending on how saucy you like it.) Cover and cook on medium-low heat until noodles are ready.

Once egg noodles are cooked, drain and return to pan. Place remaining

1 T. butter on noodles, and season to taste with salt and pepper.

Plate noodles, and top with chicken mixture. Garnish with any fresh or dried herb you have. I've used tarragon and parsley, or nothing at all.

~*~

**Linda Gordon Hengerer** writes fiction and nonfiction, including *American Football Basics*. She is currently writing the Beach Tea Shop mystery series, which takes place on the Treasure Coast of Florida. The long short story "Dying for Holiday Tea" is part of the *Happy Homicides: Thirteen Cozy Holiday Mysteries* anthology. Visit Linda at www.lindagordonhengerer.com.

## Kay Kendall's Quick Chicken and Pasta with Vegetables

Prep time: 5 min.
Cooking time: approximately 15 min.
Serves 4

12 oz. frozen pasta with chicken and sauce
1 med. onion, diced
1 cup frozen peas
12-15 ounce can chunk chicken breast

Cook frozen pasta according to package directions. Keep covered in medium-size microwave-safe dish while preparing other ingredients.

While pasta is cooking, dice onion. Combine onion and frozen peas in small bowl and microwave until cooked, about 2-3 min. or to taste.

Add canned chicken meat. Microwave 1 min. Add to bowl with pasta. Microwave an additional 1-2 min.

Season, if desired, with salt and pepper. Serve with salad and bread for a quick family dinner.

Note: You may substitute canned tuna for the canned chicken. You may also substitute other vegetables for the peas.

~*~

**Kay Kendall**'s historical mysteries capture the spirit and turbulence of the 1960s in her Austin Starr Mystery series (*Desolation Row* and *Rainy Day Women*.) A reformed PR executive whose projects won international awards, Kay lives in Texas with her Canadian husband, three house rabbits, and spaniel Wills. Degrees in Russian history and language help ground her tales in the Cold War, and her titles show she's a Bob Dylan buff. Visit Kay at www.kaykendallauthor.com.

## A.R. Kennedy's Chicken Pot Pie

Prep time: 20 min.
Cooking time: 30 min.
Serves 4

Nonstick cooking spray
1 lb. boneless skinless chicken breasts, cut into small pieces
Salt and pepper, to taste
6 oz. cream cheese
1/4 cup chicken broth
10 oz. frozen mixed vegetables
1 refrigerated piecrust

Preheat oven to 375 degrees.

Lightly coat skillet with cooking spray. Cook chicken, seasoning with salt and pepper to taste. Add cream cheese, stirring until melted. Add chicken broth and vegetables.
Simmer 5 min.

Pour mixture into deep-dish 9" pie plate. Place piecrust over mixture. Flute edges. Cut four slits along top.

Bake 30 min. or until crust is golden brown. Let stand 5 min. before serving.

~*~

**A.R. Kennedy** is the author of the Nathan Miccoli Mystery series set in New York. The latest, *Gone But Not Calm*, takes place in October 2012 when Superstorm Sandy hits. A.R. is a physical therapist, currently living in Long Beach, NY with her cute mini schnauzer, H. She's lived in nine states and traveled to over fifteen countries. She claims her greatest flaw is her love for the New York Mets. Visit A.R. at www.arkennedyauthor.com..

## Marie Laval's Quick Chicken Couscous

A delicious, tasty and nutritious dish that's very easy to prepare. This is a recipe from my mother who was born and brought up in Algeria. We used to have couscous every other Friday, and mum would invite our neighbors who were also our best friends.

Prep time: 15 min.
Cooking time: approximately 30 min.
Serves 4-5 people

2 garlic cloves, chopped
1 onion, chopped
2 T. olive oil
3 chicken breasts, cubed
3 carrots, cubed
2 sm. turnips, cubed
1/2 lb. green beans
3 sm. zucchini, cubed
1 sm. can chickpeas, rinsed in cold water (optional)
2 cups water
Pinch of salt and black pepper
1/2 tsp. each ground coriander, raz el hanout, paprika, and sweet chili (or use ready mixed couscous spices if available)
A few sprigs thyme
2 T. tomato puree
1 lb. couscous

Heat olive oil in large pan. Brown the chicken, garlic, and onion.

While chicken is cooking, clean, peel, and chop vegetables into large cubes. Snip ends of green beans and cut in half.

When chicken is golden brown, add water, vegetables, chickpeas, seasonings, and tomato puree. Cover and simmer approximately 30 min., adding more water if necessary.

While vegetables are cooking, prepare couscous according to package directions.

Serve chicken/vegetable dish over couscous.

~*~

Originally from Lyon, France, contemporary and historical romance author **Marie Laval** now lives in Lancashire, England. Being the mother of three and a full-time teacher, she's always looking for ways to find time to write. Her books include *A Spell in Provence*, *Angel Heart*, *The Lion's Embrace*, and the Dancing for the Devil trilogy. Visit Marie at www.marielaval.blogspot.co.uk.

## Claudia Lefeve's King Ranch Casserole

Prep Time: 15 min.
Cook Time: 45 min.
Servings: 6-8

It remains a mystery when and where exactly the King Ranch casserole originated, sparking much debate across kitchens for generations, but it remains a classic dish in the Texas arsenal of casseroles.

1 can cream of chicken soup
1 can cream of mushroom soup
1 cup chicken broth
1 can diced tomatoes and green chilies
1 tsp. garlic salt
Salt and pepper, to taste
1/4 cup white wine (optional)
Nonstick cooking spray
12 corn tortillas (8"), cut into quarters or strips
3 lbs. pre-cooked chicken, shredded
1 med. onion, diced
2 cups grated Mexican-blend cheese

Preheat oven to 350 degrees.

Combine cream of chicken soup, cream of mushroom soup, chicken broth, white wine, tomatoes/chilies, and all seasonings in a saucepan. Stir until warm, about 5 min. Remove from heat and set aside.

Coat a 9" x 13" baking dish with cooking spray. Place half the tortillas on bottom of pan, then layer as follows: half the chicken, half the onion, a third of the cheese. Pour half the soup mixture over the top, then repeat the layers. Add the remaining tortillas. Top with remaining cheese.
Bake 45 min. or until cheese has melted and browned slightly.

~*~

**Claudia Lefeve** was born and raised so far down the Texas Gulf Coast she has to pull out a map to show people it's nowhere near Houston. Now living in Northern Virginia, she's taking a hiatus from a civilian career in law enforcement to write mysteries full-time. She lives with her husband and three dogs. Visit Claudia at www.claudialefeve.com.

## Lisa Q. Mathews' Scarborough Maine Event Chicken

Prep time: 5 min.
Cooking time: 25-30 min.
Serves 4

I find the ingredients in this quick, 1-pan chicken dish easy to remember because the herbs are listed in the Simon and Garfunkel song "Scarborough Fair" as well as in the name of their 1966 album, *Parsley, Sage, Rosemary and Thyme*.

2 lbs. boneless chicken breasts or thigh meat, 1/4" – 1/2" thick
3 T. olive oil
8 T. yellow or 6 T. Dijon mustard (or combination of both)
1/2 pt. light cream
The following combo of fresh or dried herbs to taste (less if using dried herbs):
8 T. parsley
1/2 tsp. sage
8 T. rosemary
1 tsp. thyme
Black pepper, to taste
1 cup frozen peas (optional)

Heat olive oil in a large, heavy-bottomed sauté pan, on medium-high heat. Add all chicken pieces to pan. Coat on one side with half the mustard. Flip chicken and coat reverse side with remainder of mustard.

Lower heat if necessary. Quickly add half the herbs starting with parsley and rosemary. Flip chicken once more and sprinkle with remaining herbs.

When chicken is completely cooked, pour half the cream into the pan. Turn chicken pieces to mix the mustard and herbs with the cream, then add remaining cream.

Cover pan and allow mixture to thicken. Leave on low heat. Add optional peas. Continue to simmer until ready to serve. (Note: If sauce begins to separate, raise heat and stir, adding more cream if needed.)

~*~

**Lisa Q. Mathews** is the author of The Ladies Smythe & Westin series. The first book, *Cardiac Arrest*, will be released in November 2015, followed by *Permanently Booked* in April 2016 and *Fashionably Late* in September 2016. A former competitive figure skater, Nancy Drew editor, and mom of three grown kids, Lisa lives in New Hampshire with her husband and Willie, her crazy Golden Retriever. Visit Lisa at www.lisaqmathews.com.

## Cindy Sample's Chicken Divan

Prep time: 5-10 min.
Cooking time: 30 min.
Serves 2-3

1 sm. pkg. frozen broccoli spears
2 cups leftover chicken
10-1/2 oz. can condensed cream of chicken or chicken and mushroom soup
1/2 cup grated Parmesan cheese

Preheat oven to 325 degrees.

Cook broccoli per package instructions. Drain and place in casserole dish. Arrange chicken on top of broccoli.

Dilute soup with 1/2 can water. Pour over chicken. Sprinkle cheese on top.

Bake 30 min. or until heated through.

Option: Add your favorite spices or substitute sherry for water.

~*~

Bestselling, award-winning author **Cindy Sample** writes the Laurel McKay humorous mysteries, described as Erma Bombeck meets Agatha Christie. The series, set in the California gold country, includes *Dying for a Date, Dying for a Dance, Dying for a Daiquiri, Dying for a Dude,* and her latest release, *Dying for a Donut,* which she describes as the most fun (and most deadly) to research. Visit Cindy at www.cindysamplebooks.com.

## Sharleen Scott's Salsa Chicken Tacos

Prep time: 5 min.
Cooking time: 30-40 min.
Serves 4

Nonstick cooking spray
4 skinless, boneless chicken breasts
1 package taco seasoning
1 cup salsa
1 can fire-roasted tomatoes
1 cup cheddar cheese, plus more for topping
Tortillas
Lettuce
Olives
Canned green chilies
Tomatoes
Sour cream

Preheat oven to 375 degrees.

Halve the chicken breasts for quicker cooking. Dredge chicken breasts in taco seasoning and place in a lightly greased 13"x 9" baking dish.

Mix salsa and fire-roasted tomatoes. Pour over chicken breasts. Bake 25-35 min., or until chicken is tender and juices run clear.

Sprinkle with cheddar cheese and continue baking an additional 3-5 min.

While chicken is baking, shred lettuce and chop olives and tomatoes.

Slice or chop chicken breasts to desired size for tacos. Serve with tortillas and choice of other taco ingredients.

~*~

Romantic suspense author **Sharleen Scott** lives in the beautiful Pacific Northwest. Her Caught series (*Caught in Cross Seas* and *Caught in the Spin*), features sexy cowboys and the amazing women they love. Her latest release, *Tangles*, is a story of love, forgiveness, and redemption. It features Logan McKinnon, a man dealing with his mother's escalating Alzheimer's disease and the discovery of long buried family secrets. Book Three in the Caught series is coming in 2016. Visit Sharleen at www.sharleenscott.com.

## Joanna Campbell Slan's Curry in a Hurry

Prep time: 5 min.
Cooking time: 20 min.
Serves 4 (with rice) or 2 (if going carb-free)

1 pouch red curry simmer sauce (often in the foreign foods department)
16 oz. pre-cooked, pre-sliced chicken breast
1 pkg. frozen mixed vegetables (peppers and onion combination works well)
Rice

Start rice in rice maker or cook according to package directions.

Dump first three ingredients in large saucepan. Heat until veggies have defrosted and sauce bubbles. Reduce heat to a simmer.

When rice is finished, serve veggie/chicken sauce over rice.

~*~

**Joanna Campbell Slan** is a national bestselling author of thirty books. In her quest never to be cold again, she lives on Jupiter Island, Florida, where her neighbor, Celine Dion, almost ran over her with an SUV. Joanna writes two contemporary mysteries and one historical mystery series. Her first Kiki Lowenstein Mystery was an Agatha Award Finalist. Her historical novel starring Jane Eyre won the Daphne du Maurier Award. Visit Joanna at www.joannacampbellslan.com.

# Lynette Sofras' Lemony Roast Chicken with Shallots and Carrots

Here's a quick, delicious and inexpensive dinner recipe the whole family will love. If you like the lemony flavor, marinate the shallots and/or carrots for several hours in lemon juice before cooking.

Prep time: 5 min.
Cooking time: 30-40 min.
Serves 4

1 lb. carrots (baby carrots or large ones peeled and cut into 3" lengths)
3 oz. black olives
8-10 shallots, peeled
A few sprigs of fresh thyme
2-3 T. olive oil
8-12 chicken drumsticks
Grated zest and juice of 1-1/2 lemons
2-3 garlic cloves, finely chopped
Handful of fresh flat-leaf parsley, roughly chopped
Salt and freshly ground black pepper

Preheat oven to 400°F.

Place carrots, shallots, and olives in large roasting pan (lined with baking parchment if desired.) Drizzle with half the olive oil. Mix well to coat evenly. Sprinkle with fresh thyme.

Season the chicken drumsticks (if marinating beforehand, add seasoning to marinade) and place on top of vegetables. Drizzle with lemon juice and remaining oil.

Cook in middle of oven 30-40 min. until golden brown and cooked through. While chicken cooks, combine lemon zest, garlic, and parsley. Scatter over chicken prior to serving.

~*~

A former English teacher, **Lynette Sofras** relinquished her high level career in education to focus on her writing four years ago, thus fulfilling her lifelong dream. She mainly writes women fiction, often with suspense and/or a supernatural twist. Some of her stories include the award-winning contemporary romance *The Apple Tree*, a ghostly women's fiction, *Unworkers* and her latest romantic suspense, *The Nightclub*. Visit Lynette at www.lynettesofras.com.

## Skye Taylor's Chicken and Potato Salad

For those nights when "he" wants meat and potatoes, but you'd prefer a salad and neither of you have a lot of time.

Prep time: 10-15 min.
Cooking time: 10 min.
Serves 4

1 lb. red potatoes, cut in bite-sized chunks
1-1/4 lbs. pre-cooked boneless chicken breast
2 cups chopped romaine
2 cups baby spinach
2 scallions, sliced
Sea salt and black pepper
3 oz. feta cheese, crumbled
2 tsp. canola oil
Balsamic vinaigrette dressing

Boil potatoes until tender, 8 to 10 min.

While potatoes are cooking, cut chicken into bite-sized pieces and season with 1/2 tsp. salt and 1/2 tsp. pepper. Heat oil in wok or skillet on medium-high heat. Cook chicken 7-10 min. until cooked through.

Drain cooked potatoes and toss in a bowl with 1/3 cup vinaigrette.

Add romaine, spinach, and scallions, to potatoes; gently toss to combine. Season with salt and pepper and add additional dressing if desired. Add chicken and sprinkle with feta cheese.

~*~

**Skye Taylor** lives in the oldest city in America where she soaks up the history, takes daily walks along one of the prettiest beaches in St. Augustine, posts a weekly blog, volunteers with the USO, and writes novels. She's currently working on Book 4 in her Camerons of Tide's

Way series as well as several other projects. Her published novels include: *Whatever It Takes, Falling for Zoe, Loving Meg,* and *Trusting Will.* Visit Skye at www.skye-writer.com.

# Seafood & Fish Recipes

## Beverley Bateman's Shrimp Fajitas

Prep time: 1 min.
Cooking time: 20 min.
Serves 8

2-1/2 T. canola oil
1-1/2 lbs. lg. shrimp, shelled and deveined
6 cups peppers and onions, pre-sliced
1 T. minced garlic
1/4 cup water
6 oz. (1/2 pkg.) fajita seasoning mix
8 whole-wheat fajita-size tortillas
Reduced-fat sour cream (optional)
Salsa (optional)
Guacamole (optional)

Tip: To save on prep time purchase shrimp already shelled and deveined, bags of pre-sliced peppers and onions, a jar of minced garlic, and refrigerator guacamole.

Note: For a more complete meal, add a salad (purchased pre-made) and/or a pkg. of microwavable rice.

Heat 1 T. oil in a large stainless steel skillet. Add shrimp. Cook 3-4 min., turning once, until cooked through. Remove to a plate.

Add remaining oil, peppers, and onions to skillet. Cook 5 min., stirring occasionally, scraping up any browned bits from bottom of pan. Add garlic after 4 min.

Stir in water and seasoning mix. Cook 2 min., stirring occasionally. Return shrimp to skillet and heat through.

Serve with warm tortillas. If desired, accompany with sour cream, salsa, guacamole, rice and salad.

~*~

**Beverley Bateman** lives in the Okanagan Valley in BC, Canada among vineyards, orchards, lakes and mountains with her Shiba Inu dogs. She sits on her deck, sipping local wine and penning her latest romantic suspense novels. Books include *Hunted*, *Missing*, and *Targeted* from her Montana series; *A Cruise to Remember* and *A Murder to Forget* from her Holly Devine series; and her dark romantic suspense *Don't Go*. Visit Beverley at www.beverleybateman.com.

## Lida Bushloper's Shrimp Salad

Prep time: 10-15 min.
Cooking time: 3 min.
Serves 2

1/2 – 3/4 lb. raw shrimp
1 avocado
2 T. Thousand Island dressing

Peel shrimp. Boil 3 min. or until pink.

Drain shrimp and toss into bowl of ice water to stop cooking. This keeps the shrimp from getting tough. Drain again. Cut into small chunks.

Peel and cube avocado. Toss shrimp and avocado together with dressing.

Note: If you prefer, substitute cucumber for the avocado.

~*~

**Lida Bushloper** is a writer and poet living in Southern California. Her work has appeared in confession magazines and in academic and poetry journals, including *The Formalist* and *The Lyric*. Her mystery stories have been published in the online magazines *King's River Life*, *Mysterical-e* and *Flash Bang Mysteries*. Her volume of poetry, *Fault Lines*, was published in 2012. Visit Lida at www.lidabushloper.wordpress.com.

## Carol Goodman Kaufman's Salmon with Brussels Sprouts

This is the easiest dinner I make and among the most delicious.

Prep time: 5 min.
Cooking time: 35 min.
Serves 2

1/2 bag frozen Brussels sprouts
3/4 lb. fresh salmon filet
Salt
Pepper
Olive oil

Preheat oven to 425 degrees.

Toss sprouts in 1 T. olive oil. Sprinkle with salt and pepper.

Place in ovenproof baking pan large enough to hold both sprouts and fish. Bake 20 min.

Push sprouts to edges of pan. Place salmon filet in middle. Sprinkle 1 T. oil over top and season with salt and pepper. Cook an additional 15 min.

~*~

**Carol Goodman Kaufman,** a recovering psychologist and criminologist, writes about travel and food for regional and national newspapers and is an active blogger, tweeter, and Facebook poster. Her book, *Sins of Omission*, looks at communal response to domestic violence. She is at work on a food history *cum* cookbook and a murder mystery in which food plays a role. Visit Carol at www.carolgoodmankaufman.com.

## Joanne Guidoccio's Quick 'n' Easy Halibut

Prep time: 5 min.
Cooking time: 15 min.
Serves 4

4 halibut fillets (about 1-1/2 lbs.)
1/4 tsp. salt
1/4 tsp. black pepper
1 tsp. chervil
1 T. lemon juice
1/4 cup margarine

Arrange fillets in a microwaveable dish. Sprinkle with salt, black pepper, and chervil. Drizzle with lemon juice.

Cover tightly with plastic wrap and microwave on high 8-10 min. or until fish flakes easily with fork. Rotate the dish after 4 min.

Let the fillets stand covered 3 min. Drain.

Melt the margarine in the microwave, using medium heat, 1-2 min. Pour over fish before serving.

~*~

In 2008 **Joanne Guidoccio** took advantage of early retirement and launched a writing career. When she tried her hand at fiction, she made reinvention a recurring theme in her novels and short stories. Joanne writes cozy mysteries and paranormal romance from her home base of Guelph, Ontario. Her novels include *A Season for Killing Blondes*, *Between Land and Sea*, and *The Coming of Arabella*. Visit Joanne at www.joanneguidoccio.com.

## Margaret S. Hamilton's Garides Tourkolimano (Greek Shrimp)

Prep time: 10 min.
Cooking time: approximately 12 min.
Serves 2

1 T. olive oil
1 lb. shrimp, peeled and deveined (frozen is fine)
4 cloves garlic, chopped
1 lg. tomato, chopped (or 14.5 oz can diced tomatoes)
4 green onions, sliced
1/2 cup white wine
1 tsp. oregano
1/4 cup fresh basil, chopped
1 bay leaf
Salt and pepper
1/2 lb. feta cheese
2 T. fresh parsley, chopped

Heat olive oil in pan, sauté shrimp 1 min. on each side and remove. Sauté garlic 1 min. Add tomato and green onion. Sauté 3-5 min. Add shrimp, wine, herbs, and seasonings. Simmer 2 min.

Remove from heat and mix in crumbled feta. Cover and rest 3 min. Sprinkle with parsley. Serve with bread.

~*~

**Margaret S. Hamilton** has published short stories in the *Darkhouse Destination: Mystery!* anthology and *Kings River Life*. She also writes traditional mystery novels. Visit Margaret at www.margaretshamilton.wordpress.com.

## Kathryn Jane's Mom's Salmon Cakes

When I was a kid, my grandfather, who was a cannery engineer, sent my family a box of canned salmon. It was like gold, so Mom used it sparingly and here's one of her recipes. Now I serve it with a simple baked potato when I'm in a hurry. (Takes about a minute to scrub a couple of spuds, poke holes in them, and toss them in oven.)

Prep time: 5-10 min.
Cooking time: 15-20 min.
Serves 4-6

6-8 oz. canned salmon
3 eggs
1/2 T. flour
1/4 tsp. salt
Pepper, to taste
Butter or oil for the pan

Separate eggs.

Mix salmon (crush and use all the contents, including bones and skin,) egg yolks, flour, salt and pepper in a large bowl.

Beat egg whites until stiff. Fold egg whites into salmon mixture. For maximum puffiness, be very gentle.

Heat a small amount of butter or oil in pan or griddle on medium heat.

Drop salmon mixture by spoonfuls into heated pan. Smooth out slightly to create an even thickness. Cook until a nice crust forms on bottom, then flip to heat reverse side. If you prefer non-crispy salmon cakes, cover pan while cooking.

~*~

Addicted to the ocean and the color turquoise, award-winning author

**Kathryn Jane** lives on the west coast of Canada with an obnoxious cat and a faithful dog, who keeps the man of her dreams company while she's busy penning fast-paced mysteries and adventures about kick-ass women and the men who dare to love them. Visit Kathryn at www.kathrynjane.com.

## Lynn Kinnaman's Cod Under Wraps

Prep time: 15 min.
Cooking time: 20 min.
Serves 2

2 cod fillets
6 onion slices, about a 1/3" thick
1 carrot, sliced into 2" long matchsticks
3 green onions, sliced into 2" long matchsticks
1 T. olive oil
1/2 T. butter, melted
1 T. lemon juice
Asian seasoning (optional)
Foil, heavy-duty or doubled

Preheat oven to 350 degrees.

Cut two pieces of heavy foil large enough to wrap the fish airtight when folded over. Place 3 onion slices on each piece of foil. Lay cod on top of onions. Then divide carrots and green onions over fish. Lift the foil up on all sides to trap olive oil mixture in next step.

Whisk olive oil, butter, and lemon juice together. Add optional Asian seasoning to taste. Pour half over each piece of fish piece. Fold foil and secure tightly.

Bake approximately 15 min., depending on the thickness of fish. If cod is thin, cooking time will be less. Fish is done when it flakes or reaches internal temperature of 145 degrees. Unwrap carefully to avoid burns from the steam.

~*~

**Lynn Kinnaman** is published in both fiction and nonfiction. Her current passion is a cozy mystery series about Leah Clark, a woman who discovers she has a talent for finding trouble and a knack for solving crimes in her travels. Lynn enjoys spending time with her family, cooking, and venturing forth to find her own adventures in her travel-trailer, accompanied by her canine companion, an opinionated Jack Russell named Sadie. Visit Lynn at www.lynnkinnaman.com.

## B.V. Lawson's Foil Flounder

One of my absolute favorite quick recipes is baked fish in foil. It's not only healthy, it's easy to make and easy to clean up.

Prep time: 5 min.
Cooking time: 20-25 min.
Serves 2

1 med. zucchini, chopped
1 med. yellow squash, chopped
1 med. onion, chopped
2 flounder fillets (approximately 1/2 lb. each)
Italian seasoning

Preheat oven to 350 degrees.

Place vegetables on a large piece of aluminum foil. (Buying pre-chopped vegetables saves prep time.) Top with flounder filets. Drizzle with olive oil, and sprinkle with Italian seasoning.

Fold up the sides of the foil and close the packet tightly. Bake approximately 20-25 min.

~*~

**B.V. Lawson** is an author, poet, and journalist whose writing has appeared in dozens of publications. She's also a four-time Derringer Award finalist and 2012 winner for her short fiction. B.V.'s debut novel, *Played to Death*, was named Best Mystery in the 2015 Next Generation Indie Book Awards and a Shamus Award finalist. She lives in Virginia with her husband and enjoys flying above the Chesapeake Bay in a little Cessna. Visit B.V. at www.bvlawson.com.

## Elizabeth Rose's Grilled Salmon

My heroine, Cassie Briggs from *The Caretaker of Showman's Hill* cooks this meal for Basil Wensilton III, not realizing he's a vampire.

Prep time: 10 min.
Cooking time: 15-20 min.
Serves 2

6" tailpiece fresh salmon, skin on.
Extra virgin olive oil
Toasted sesame ginger dressing
Cayenne pepper or paprika
Nonstick spray
2 cloves fresh garlic, minced
1/2 tsp. fresh ginger, minced
1 tsp. fresh turmeric root, grated

Cut salmon in half. Brush olive oil on both pink side and skin side to prevent sticking to grill.

Brush dressing on pink side of salmon. Sprinkle with cayenne or paprika.

Spray grill grates. Heat grill to medium. Place salmon skin-side down on the grill. Cook 15-20 min. (Time depends on thickness of salmon and temperature of grill.)

The last 2 minutes of grilling, flip the salmon so it'll get nice grill marks. The skin side may look burnt but just remove it before eating.

For sauce, mix together 4-6 T. of the sesame ginger dressing, the garlic, ginger, and turmeric. The turmeric root will give the sauce a tangy kick, and the fresh ginger gives a blast of spice.

Serve salmon topped with the sauce over bed of rice and with a vegetable side dish that you cook while salmon is grilling.

~*~

**Elizabeth Rose** is a bestselling author of over forty-five romance novels, ranging from historicals to contemporaries to paranormals and westerns. Her medieval series include Daughters of the Dagger, Legacy of the Blade, MadMan MacKeefe, and The Barons of the Cinque Ports. She also writes The Tarnished Saints small-town contemporary series about the twelve brothers of a preacher. Visit Elizabeth at www.elizabethrosenovels.com.

## Lea Wait's Tuna Pasta Salad

Prep time: 10 min.
Cooking time: 10 min.
Serves: 4

1 lb. macaroni
3 T. olive oil
12 oz. canned tuna fish
1 stalk celery, chopped
3 scallions, chopped
1/2 cup red onion, chopped
1 cup green olives with pimento, chopped
2/3 cup mayonnaise or mayonnaise substitute
Salt, black pepper, and cayenne, to taste

Bring large pot of salted water and olive oil to boil. Add macaroni and cook according to package directions.

While macaroni is cooking, chop all ingredients as listed and mix with tuna, mayonnaise, and seasonings in large salad bowl.

Add cooked macaroni to salad bowl. Serve hot or cold.

Maine author **Lea Wait** writes the Shadows Antique Print and the Mainely Needlepoint mystery series. Recent titles include *Threads of Evidence* and *Shadows of a Maine Christmas*. She's also the author of historical novels for children ages 8 and up and has penned a memoir, *Living and Writing on the Coast of Maine*. Visit Lea at www.leawait.com.

## Regan Walker's Baked Salmon Salad

I rarely have time to cook, and after a long day of research and writing historical romance, I'm tired and hungry. I just want a quick, healthy meal. This dish is a staple for me. I typically eat it twice a week. The time saving tips make preparation quick.

Prep time: 5 minutes
Cooking time: 15-20 minutes
Serves 1 (or more, depending on size of salmon)

Salmon
Your choice of spices/herbs/seasonings
Salad greens
Other salad vegetables (any variety)
Salad toppings (your choice)
Salad dressing (your choice)

Preheat the oven to 375 degrees.

While oven is heating, assemble the salad: lettuce, veggies and goodies. I use a chopper because I like my salad greens fine. Toss the salad but don't add the dressing yet.

Line the baking pan with foil so you can toss the foil at the end and have a clean pan. Spray foil with olive oil. (I use a Misto oil sprayer filled with my favorite olive oil, but you can also buy commercial olive oil spray.)

Place salmon in pan. Coat with your choice of spices/herbs/seasonings.

Bake 15-20 min., depending on the thickness of your salmon.

When the salmon is cooked, add the dressing to the salad and toss. Turn the salad onto a dinner plate and place the salmon on top of it.
Options: If you have time, you can grill the salmon. You can also

substitute chicken or make a vegetarian option with an avocado and crumbled goat cheese.

To save time buy a large piece of fresh salmon (any variety.) Cut into smaller pieces and freeze individually. Just remember to remove from the freezer ahead of time to thaw before cooking.

Buy enough lettuce or packaged salad greens for several salads. If they need to be washed, do so ahead of time and place in plastic bags stored in your refrigerator veggie drawer.

Keep a variety of salad toppings such as dried cranberries and glazed pecans on hand.

~*~

Bestselling historical romance author **Regan Walker** incorporates actual events and real people in her adventurous tales that span from medieval times through the Georgian period. Among her titles are *The Red Wolf's Prize* and *Rogue Knight* from her Medieval Warriors series and *To Tame the Wind* and *Racing with the Wind* from her Agents of the Crown series. She's also written three holiday stories. Visit Regan at www.reganwalkerauthor.com.

# Soup, Stew & Chili Recipes

## Cori Lynn Arnold's Coming Home to Warm Minestrone

Want a warm dish that doesn't taste like it's been sitting in a slow cooker for 8 hours? Learn to use your oven's delay start. I promise, like recording your favorite show with an old VCR, it's tough to figure out at first, but the results will be worth it.

During the school year, I am practically a full-time taxi driver. Three to four days a week I drive my son to his athletic practices about 20 miles away. Most of the time it only takes me 20 min., but sometimes (Fridays!) it's more like an hour. We get home pretty late, and we need a warm, nourishing meal when we arrive. I make this minestrone, and almost every soup or casserole I make, in double or triple batches and save time by plopping the contents of a 2 qt. bag from the freezer into a Dutch oven and delay starting my oven before I leave, so that it's warm and delicious when we walk through the door.

Prep time: 10 min.
Cooking time: 30 min.
Serves 6-8

1 med. onion, chopped
2 cloves garlic
2 T. olive oil
1-1/2 cups potatoes, cubed
1 cup carrots, cubed
2 cups zucchini, cubed
1 cup green beans, cut into 1" lengths
1 cup cabbage, chopped
2 T. of Italian seasoning (or a mix of parsley, rosemary, thyme)
Salt and pepper, to taste
4 cups stock, vegetable or chicken
16 oz. canned beans (any variety,) rinsed
16 oz. can stewed tomatoes

2 cups cooked pasta (any variety)

Sauté the onions and garlic in olive oil 2 min. in a large pot on medium heat. Toss in potatoes, carrots, zucchini, green beans, and cabbage, sautéing another 10 min. Stir in Italian seasoning, salt and pepper.

Add stock, beans, and tomatoes. Heat to boiling. Simmer, covered, 10 min. Add cooked pasta.

At this point the soup is ready to serve, but it will taste so much better once the soup has had time to meld together. Let the soup cool and place in 2-qt. freezer bags and freeze. Also, leave a little in the fridge and watch it disappear!

To reheat: Empty contents of 2-qt. freezer bag into lidded Dutch oven. Heat 2-1/2 – 3 hrs. at 350 degrees using the delay start feature of your oven in order to have your minestrone hot and ready when you get home.

~*~

**Cori Lynn Arnold** has worked as a housekeeper, library clerk, photographic archivist, tutor, artwork framer, portrait and wedding photographer, high school algebra teacher, Internet security researcher, security analyst, computer programmer and ethical hacker. She grew up in North Pole, Alaska where her latest mystery, *Northern Deceit*, is set. Her thriller, *Thin Luck*, will come out in 2016. She currently resides in West Hartford, Connecticut and works as a part-time mother and full time author. Visit Cori at www.facebook.com/CoriLynnArnold.

## Lesley A. Diehl's Santa Fe White Chili

Prep time: 10 min.
Cooking time: less than 30 min.
Serves 4

1-1/2 tsp. garlic powder
1-1/2 tsp. cumin
3/4 tsp. dried oregano
1 T. olive oil (use more if desired)
1 – 1-1/4 lbs. boneless, skinless chicken breasts, cubed
1/2 cup onion, chopped
14-1/2 oz. fat-free chicken broth
4-1/2 oz. can chopped green chilies (not jalapeno chilies)
1 bay leaf
30 oz. canned cannelloni beans (rinse and drain if you like)
Shredded Monterey Jack cheese
Scallions, sliced (optional)

Combine garlic powder, cumin, and oregano in a small dish and blend. Set aside.

Heat oil over medium heat in a large nonstick skillet or Dutch oven. Add chicken and onion. Cook until chicken is lightly browned, stirring often.

Stir in chicken broth, chilies, mixed spices, and bay leaf. Simmer on low heat 15 min. Stir in beans and simmer an additional 5 min. Remove bay leaf.

Top with garnish of cheese and optional scallions before serving.

~*~

**Lesley A. Diehl** spends her summers in upstate New York where a shy ghost serves as her literary muse and her winters in Florida where gators make golf a contact sport. She's the author of the Microbrewing

Mysteries, the Big Lake Mysteries, the Eve Appel Mysteries, and the Laura Murphy Mysteries as well as the stand alone mystery *Angel Sleuth*, and numerous short stories. Visit Lesley at www.lesleyadiehl.com.

## Jennifer Faye's Stuffed Pepper Soup

Timesaving recipes for me are healthy meals that will feed the family for at least two nights. Leftovers are my friends. And I like to share extras with my extended family.

Prep time: 15-20 min.
Cooking time: 75 min.
Serves 10

2 lbs. lean ground beef (the leaner, the better)
2 med. onions, diced
3 peppers, diced (any variety or a combination)
58 oz. canned diced tomatoes
24 oz. tomato sauce
12 oz. canned mushrooms
32 oz. low sodium beef broth
3 cups cooked Minute Rice
2 cups water
1 T. garlic powder
1 T. onion powder
1 T. basil
1 T. Italian seasoning
2 cloves garlic, minced
Salt and pepper, to taste

In a large soup pot, brown the beef. Add the minced onion and garlic. Cook until the onion is tender, approximately 5 min.

Add the diced tomatoes, tomato sauce, mushrooms, broth and seasoning. Bring to a boil. Cover. Simmer 1 hr., stirring occasionally.

Add the water and rice. Continue to cook another 10 min. Remove from heat and serve.

~*~

Award-winning author **Jennifer Faye** pens fun, heartwarming contemporary romances. She's a two-time winner of the *RT Book Reviews* Reviewers' Choice Award as well as a mom to two very spoiled cats. Her Whistle Stop Romance series features lots of small-town quirky characters. Titles include *A Moment to Love*, *A Moment to Dance*, and *A Moment on the Lips* with more to come. Visit Jennifer at www.jenniferfaye.com.

## Flo Fitzpatrick's Easy Texas Chili

Prep time: 5 min.
Cooking time: 40 min.
Serves 4

1 lb. ground beef
1 can diced tomatoes and green chilies
1 can dark red kidney beans
Chili powder, to taste
Cumin, to taste
Garlic, to taste (use garlic salt or minced from jar)
1 cup rice, uncooked
Shredded 4-cheese Mexican mix or Monterey Jack with peppers cheese

Follow package instructions to cook rice. Double the recipe if you want leftovers.

While rice is cooking, brown the meat. Mix in can of tomatoes/green chilies and beans. Add remainder of ingredients. Simmer approximately 30 min. Turn burner down to low until ready to serve.

Pour chili over rice. Sprinkle with cheese.

If you're not in the mood for the chili flavor, skip the beans and the chili powder and cumin and pour the meat mixture over cooked pasta.

~*~

**Flo Fitzpatrick** is a multi-published author of mystery, romance and paranormals (sometimes within the same book.) She often draws on her background as a performer and choreographer to create wacky characters. Her latest release is *Pick up the Pieces*. The paranormal *Scarecrow's Dream* will be a 2016 release. Currently living in Alabama, Flo sings with the jazz band The Usual Suspects, noting "....Moondance" (the title of a paranormal released in 2010) is also her signature song. Visit Flo at www.flofitzpatrick.com.

## L.C. Hayden's Half-Hour Chili Con Carne

Prep time: 5 min.
Cooking time: 25-30 min.
Serves 4-6

Med. onion or 3 T. minced onion
1 sm. jalapeno or 1/3 tsp. crushed red pepper (optional)
1 lb. ground beef or ground turkey
1/2 tsp. garlic powder
1/2 tsp. Mrs. Dash (I normally use the Table Blend)
1/2 tsp. oregano
1/2 cup barbeque sauce
1/4 cup ketchup
1 can beans (any variety)
1 can condensed tomato soup
1 cup milk

If using fresh onion and jalapeno, chop them, brown them, and set aside. Using a large saucepot, brown the ground beef or turkey until well done. Add ingredients in the order mentioned above, stopping before adding the beans, soup, and milk. Stir well and simmer 3 min., then add the beans, soup, and milk. Cook on low heat, removing from burner just as mixture begins to boil.

Serve with a side salad and fresh bread.

Hint: some people like it hot, others not so hot. I normally don't add the crushed red pepper while cooking. I allow each person to decide how much to add.

~*~

Bestselling author **L.C. Hayden** writes the popular Bronson and Brent series. Her newest release is *Secrets of the Tunnels*. Hayden's awards include being an Agatha nominee, and winning Left Coast Crime's Best

Regional Mystery, Watson Award, and Best of the Best Award. A popular speaker, she's presented writing workshops at major cruise lines while cruising all over the world. Visit L.C. at www.lchayden.com.

## R. Franklin James' Ready for Anything Stew

For me, meal timesavers involve one pot and producing multiple servings or days worth of meals. I adapted this soup/stew recipe to not only address simple preparation but healthy eating. A great Fall/Winter/Spring dish.

Prep Time: 30 min. or less
Cooking time: 3-6 hrs.
Serves 6-7

1 box chicken broth
28 oz. canned crushed tomatoes
1 onion, chopped
2 stalks celery, chopped
2 carrots, chopped
1 green pepper, chopped
2 potatoes, chopped
1 turnip, chopped
1 cabbage, chopped
1-1/2 lbs. stew meat, cut into 1" pieces
2-3 bay leaves
Crushed red pepper, to taste
Salt and pepper, to taste
Italian seasoning, to taste
Garlic powder, to taste
Turmeric, to taste

Fill large pot with chicken broth and crushed tomatoes. Place under medium-low flame. Add chopped vegetables and stew meat. Feel free to add other vegetables not listed or use frozen vegetables but add them toward the end of the meat cooking.

After the contents reach a simmer, add seasonings. Cook all day (at least 5-6 hrs. on low) or a minimum of 3 hrs. on medium. I put it on in the morning, and go back to writing. The aroma is fantastic.

Serve with corn muffins or hard rolls.

Note: If you work outside the home, place all ingredients in a slow cooker before you leave the house in the morning. Cook on low all day. Dinner will be ready when you return from work.

**R. Franklin James** followed a career of political advocacy with writing mysteries. Her debut novel, *The Fallen Angels Book Club*, the first book in her Hollis Morgan Mystery series, was published in 2013. *Sticks & Stones* and *The Return of the Fallen Angels Book Club* followed. The fourth book in the series, *The Trade List*, will be a May 2016 release. Visit R. Franklin at www.rfranklinjames.com.

## Gemma Juliana's Peas Purée

Peas are polarizing. You'll rarely find someone middle-of-the-road about peas. I love peas! Here's a fast and delicious way to enjoy these sweet little green balls...peas, if you please.

Prep time: 5 min.
Cooking time: 10 min.
Serves 2 as a main dish or 4 as a side dish

1 clove garlic, crushed
Himalayan salt
White pepper
16 oz. frozen peas
6 T. crème fraiche or heavy cream
6 T. grated Parmesan cheese
2 tsp. dried mint or 2 tsp. mint jelly
Dollop of grass-fed butter (optional)

Add salt to 1/2 cup cold water in a pan and crush the garlic into it. Bring to a boil and add peas.

Cook 5-7 min. until tender. Drain.

Use a blender or an old-fashioned potato masher to puree the peas with crème fraiche, mint, and Parmesan cheese. It will look curdled. Add salt and white pepper to taste. Top with optional butter.

Tip: This can easily be turned into soup by adding 16 oz. chicken or vegetable broth. It also can be blended with buttered mashed potatoes and topped with a fried egg.

~*~

Author **Gemma Juliana** writes romance and mystery in various sub-genres from contemporary to paranormal. Her current focus is international love stories. When not at her desk, Gemma loves cooking for family and friends, collecting feathers, sticks and sparkly stones, and traveling the world. Her muse demands large doses of coffee and chocolate. Gemma's titles include *Riviera Rendezvous, Autumn Masquerade, Christmas Spirits, The Sheikh's Spy, To Kiss a Leprechaun,* and many more. Visit Gemma at www.gemmajuliana.com.

## Alice Loweecey's Corn and Sausage Chowder

Prep time: 10 min.
Cooking time: 25 min.
Serves 6

1 lb. bulk pork sausage
1 cup onion, chopped
4 cups potatoes, skins on and cubed
1/2 tsp. salt
1/2 tsp. dried marjoram, crushed
1/8 tsp. pepper
2 cups water
The kernels from 3-4 fresh ears of corn (if it's the wrong season, substitute 1 can whole-kernel corn, drained, and 1 can cream-style corn)
12 oz. can evaporated milk

In a large pot, cook the sausage and onion until the sausage is brown and the onion is tender. Drain grease.

Add potatoes, salt, pepper, marjoram, and water. If using fresh corn, add in at this point. Bring to boiling; reduce heat and simmer until potatoes are tender, about 15 min.

Add evaporated milk. If using canned corn, add it now. Heat through.

~*~

Baker of brownies and tormenter of characters, **Alice Loweecey** recently celebrated her thirtieth year outside the convent. She grew up watching Hammer horror films and Scooby-Doo mysteries, which explains a whole lot. When she's not creating trouble for her sleuth Giulia Driscoll or inspiring nightmares as her alter ego Kate Morgan, she can be found growing her own vegetables (in summer) and cooking with them (the rest of the year). Visit Alice at www.aliceloweecey.net.

## Cynthia Luhrs' Sneaky Tomato Soup

I'm always on the lookout for ways to add more veggies and legumes to my diet. This soup covers all the bases, tastes great, and fills you up. Serve with a salad and you have a quick, easy meal.

Prep Time: 7 min.
Cooking Time: 15 min. (7 min. if you have a high speed blender like a Vitamix)
Serves 6

1/2 cup onion, chopped
1 T. minced garlic
4 cups broth, vegetable or chicken
2 T. lemon juice
14 oz. can diced tomatoes
15 oz. can chickpeas, drained and rinsed
2 tsp. oregano
2 tsp. parsley
1/8 cup olive oil
Salt and pepper, to taste

Add first 6 ingredients to a pot and bring to a boil. Add the oregano, parsley, and olive oil. Season with salt and pepper.

Blend with immersion blender or regular blender.

Alternate directions for Vitamix: Add the ingredients to the container in the order listed. Make sure lid is on tight. Start on low then quickly increase speed to 10, then high. Blend on high 7 min. or until steam escapes from the vented lid.

Note: If you prefer a chunky soup, reserve half the tomatoes and chickpeas. Add them at the end and blend 5 seconds to roughly chop or leave as is for extra chunky soup.

~*~

**Cynthia Luhrs** is the author of the ghostly Shadow Walker novels and the Merriweather Sisters Time Travel novels, featuring sassy heroines in medieval England. Her idea of a perfect day is no interruptions and the freedom to live in her head all day, writing to her heart's content, a glass of sweet tea next to her as she creates the next book. Of course her tiger cats frequently disrupt this oasis of serenity. Visit Cynthia at www.cluhrs.com.

## Sandra McGregor's Hamburger Helper Soup

Prep time: under 5 min.
Cooking time: 20-25 min.
Serves 4

Note: You may want to double the recipe; people will want more.

1 lb. hamburger, fried and drained
1 box Hamburger Helper, any flavor
5 cups water
15 oz. can chopped tomatoes
1 can whole-kernel corn
1 zucchini, sliced thin, or 1 can green beans

Bring water, prepared hamburger, Hamburger Helper flavor packet, tomatoes and canned vegetables to a boil. Add zucchini and Hamburger Helper noodles. Simmer 5 min. Serve.

~*~

**Sandra McGregor** sold her first book eight years after her husband issued her a challenge not to wait until retirement to begin writing. Sandra has published two sweet contemporary novels as Sandra Elzie and thirteen as Sandra McGregor. Some of her titles include *Behind Door Two, Dad Next Door, Pennies on The Dollar*, the Duty series, the Templeton series, the Dawn series, and the upcoming Harrington series. Visit Sandra at www.sandramcgregor.blogspot.com.

## Stacey Joy Netzel's Slow Cooker Chicken Chili

A perfect set-it-and-forget-it meal! It also freezes well for future meals.

Prep time: 15 min.
Cook time: 7-8 hrs.
Serves 6-8

30 oz. canned petite diced tomatoes, undrained
48 oz. jar great northern beans, undrained
30 oz. canned black beans, drained
24-36 oz. salsa
1 pkg. chili or taco seasoning
4 med. uncooked boneless chicken breasts, trimmed (or frozen)
Sour cream
Shredded cheddar cheese
Tortilla chips

Mix first 6 ingredients together in a large slow cooker. Cook on low for 7 or more hrs., with chicken breasts submerged in rest of ingredients.

Before serving, shred chicken with a fork or potato masher right in the slow cooker. Serve with sour cream, shredded cheddar cheese and tortilla chips.

~*~

*New York Times* bestselling author **Stacey Joy Netzel** is an avid reader and loves all movies with a happily ever after. She lives in Wisconsin with her family, a horse, and some barn cats. In her free time she enjoys gardening, canning, and visiting her parents in Northeastern Wisconsin (Up North), at the family lake cabin. Her bestselling books include the Romancing Wisconsin Series, Italy Intrigue Series, Welcome to Redemption Series, and Colorado Trust Series. Visit Stacey at www.staceyjoynetzel.com.

## Jayne Ormerod's Chicken and Noodles Soup

Prep time: about 10 min.
Cook time: approximately 2-1/2 hrs.
Serves 4-6

1 whole chicken, cut up (or 4 bone-in chicken breasts)
2 cans chicken broth
Water
Salt and pepper
1 lb. bag med. egg noodles

In a large pot, place chicken, broth, two cans of water and salt and pepper (I use about 1 tsp. each, but I love a peppery flavor.) Bring to a boil. Reduce heat, and simmer, covered, 2 hrs. (Use this time wisely to write or promote your latest release.)

Turn off heat and remove chicken from broth. Cut chicken from bones (discarding bones,) then cut or shred chicken into bite-size pieces. Return chicken to pot.

Bring to a boil. Stir in noodles and cook according to package directions.

Serve with crusty bread and a salad.

~*~

**Jayne Ormerod** grew up in a small Ohio town, then went on to a small-town Ohio college. Upon earning her degree in accountancy she became a CIA (That's not a sexy spy thing, but a Certified Internal Auditor.) She married a naval officer, and off they sailed to see the world. After fifteen moves she realized she needed a more transportable vocation, so she began writing cozy mysteries. *Blond Faith* is her latest release. Visit Jayne at www.jayneormerod.com.

# Pepper Phillips' Shrimp and Corn Soup

Prep time: 1 min.
Cooking time: less than 10 min.
Serves 4-6

This recipe keeps well in the refrigerator. So make a double batch and serve again later in the week.

10-1/2 oz. can cream of potato soup
10-1/2 oz. heavy duty whipping cream or half and half (use empty soup can for measuring)
15 oz. can whole kernel corn
15 oz. can creamed corn
12 oz. pkg. pre-cooked, deveined, tail-off shrimp (defrost if frozen)
Cajun seasoning, to taste

Place the cream of potato soup in a 4 qt. saucepan. Add the cream or half and half, stirring until smooth.

Add both cans of corn. Do not drain the whole kernel corn.
Heat to a bubbling stage and add the shrimp. Add the Cajun seasoning to taste.

Once the mixture bubbles again, it's finished. If soup seems too thick, add more cream or half and half.

Serve with crackers, garlic bread or cornbread.

~*~

According to author **Pepper Phillips**, she's older than dirt, a cliché but true since she married as a mere child. She somehow managed to raise six kids without killing any of them. Her thirteen grandkids are all fantastic and gorgeous because they're her descendants, and her hubby is still around because both of them are too tired to pack up and move out. Pepper tells stories...with a basis of truth and maybe some lies. Visit

Pepper at www.pepperphillips.com.

## Susan C. Shea's Fresh Chicken Vegetable Soup

A favorite quick, homemade soup, exceptionally low in calories and high in nutrition and taste. If you want to add a starch, throw in a little pre-cooked rice or noodles near the finish, but don't cook them in the stock or you'll soak up too much liquid. This recipe is mostly assemblage, with some meditative work at the cutting board.

Prep time: 10 min.
Cooking time: 20-30 min.
Serves 2-4

1 qt. low-sodium organic chicken stock
2 organic half chicken breasts
1/2 lb. fresh green beans
3 carrots
1 sm. head bok choy (can substitute broccoli cut into small florets or thinly sliced zucchini)
1 sweet red pepper
2/3 cup frozen baby peas
2" peeled fresh ginger
2-3 green onions
1-2 garlic cloves
Soy sauce

Cut the chicken into 1" pieces.

Finely chop ginger and garlic.

Bring stock to a gentle boil, add the chicken, ginger and garlic. Turn burner to simmer and cook 3-4 min. until chicken is cooked through but tender.

While chicken is cooking, cut up green beans, carrots and bok choy.

Dice the red pepper and green onions (I use both white and green parts.) Add the beans and carrots to the stock. Then, add the bok choy, frozen peas, red pepper, and onions.

Add a little water to replace what's boiled off the stock. Add soy sauce to taste and remove from heat immediately so the veggies don't overcook. You want color and a bit of crispness. I sometimes add a bit of dried chili peppers.

Salt and pepper, to taste.

~*~

**Susan C. Shea** spent more than two decades accumulating story material before creating her bestselling mystery series featuring a professional fundraiser for a fictional museum in San Francisco. Titles include *Murder in the Abstract*, *The King's Jar*, and the upcoming *Mixed Up with Murder*. She's currently the president of the northern California chapter of Sisters in Crime and on SinC's national board. Visit Susan at www.susancshea.com.

## Kaye Spencer's Hamburger Goulash

Prep time: 10 min.
Cooking time: 20 min.
Serves 6-10 (depending upon size of appetites)

1-2 lbs. ground beef
12 oz. pkg. extra wide egg noodles
30 oz. (more or less) tomato sauce
2 cups (more or less) shredded cheddar cheese
Garlic powder
Onion powder
Chili powder
Salt
Parmesan cheese, freshly grated or from container (optional)
Dry oregano (optional)

Prepare noodles according to directions on package.

While the noodles are cooking, thoroughly brown the ground beef in a large skillet. Drain well.

Drain cooked noodles and return to cooking pot. Stir in browned ground beef. Stir in a generous shake of salt, garlic powder, onion powder, and chili powder to taste. Add tomato sauce until you like the consistency—not runny, not sticky.

Turn the burner to low and stir in the shredded cheddar cheese until the mixture warms and the cheese begins to melt. Stir gently, but frequently to prevent the goulash from scorching.

Sprinkle with optional Parmesan cheese and/or oregano after plating. Serve with garlic bread (the kind packaged in foil from the freezer section) and vegetable of choice.

~*~

A prairie girl at heart, native Coloradan **Kaye Spencer** writes sweet to spicy historical romances, most of which are set in the Old West. Kaye refers to herself as a lover of words, crafter of stories, and a hopelessly hopeful romantic. Visit Kaye at www.kayespencer.wordpress.com.

## Lourdes Venard's White Bean Stew

Prep time: 10-15 min.
Cooking time: approximately 40 min.
Serves 4

This is a quick recipe that my husband and I eat as a main dish. We find it very filling, especially when served with bruschetta or any nice bread. It can also be used as a side dish.

2-3 slices bacon
3 garlic cloves, minced
1/2 tsp. crushed red pepper flakes (this can be very spicy, so put in less if you want a milder dish)
1 cup onion, diced
1 bag spinach or 1 lb. uncooked kale, stemmed
1 cup chicken broth
15-oz. can cannellini beans, rinsed and drained
1 tsp. salt
1 T. balsamic vinegar
1 tsp. sugar

Cook bacon in a skillet. Remove bacon and set aside, leaving drippings in skillet. Add garlic and red pepper flakes to drippings and cook 30 sec. – 1 min. Add onion and cook an additional 10 min.

Add kale or spinach, stirring until it begins to wilt, about 5-7 min. add broth and cover. Simmer over low heat 8-10 min. until kale is tender, less time if using spinach.

Add beans and simmer uncovered 5-7 min.

Stir in salt, vinegar, and sugar. Crumble bacon. Sprinkle on top of stew.

~*~

**Lourdes Venard** is founder of Comma Sense Editing, which provides services to individual authors and businesses. She has thirty years of writing and editing experience, including at *Newsday*, *The Miami Herald*, *Chicago Tribune*, *Milwaukee Journal Sentinel*, and *The Washington Post*. She also teaches copyediting through an online course at the University of California, San Diego, and authored *Publishing for Beginning: What First-Time Authors Need to Know*. Visit Lourdes at www.commasense.net.

# Vegetarian & Miscellaneous Recipes

## Lisa Alber's Slow Cooker Delish Vegan Enchilada Casserole

Prep time: 10 min.
Cooking time: 4-5 hrs.
Serves 6-8

Nonstick cooking spray or slow cooker liner
1 lg. yam, thinly sliced
24 oz. enchilada sauce
1 bag corn tortillas
12 oz. soy chorizo
30 oz. canned black beans, drained and rinsed

Oil the slow cooker or use a liner. Thinly coat the bottom with enchilada sauce. Layer the ingredients in the following order, three times: corn tortillas, chorizo, yam slices, beans, enchilada sauce. Add a final layer of corn tortillas and the remaining enchilada sauce.

Cook on low 4-5 hrs. This recipe is safe to leave on low longer if you plan to be away from home all day.

Variations: This recipe is very versatile. You can swap out the vegetarian chorizo for meat chorizo and also add layers of shredded cheese of your choice. For more vegetables, try adding spinach, zucchini, onions, olives, or mushrooms. For a gluten-free vegetarian alternative, use tofu in place of the soy chorizo.

~*~

**Lisa Alber** is the author of *Kilmoon*, an atmospheric mystery set in Ireland that has been described as "utterly poetic" and a "stirring debut," and *Whispers in the Mist*. She's an Elizabeth George Foundation writing grant and Walden Fellowship recipient. Some of her favorite things include travel, photography, her pets, coffee shops, puttering around the yard, red wine, Sunday afternoon naps, spooky movies, the color teal, and her mom's tuna casserole. Visit Lisa at www.lisaalber.com.

## Reggi Allder's Vegetarian California Chef's Salad with a Spicy Twist

Prep time: approximately 30 min.
Cooking time: 5-10 min.
Serves 4

1 head iceberg lettuce
1 head romaine lettuce
2-3 stalks scallions, cut into small pieces. (Use both white and green part)
1 bell pepper, diced
3 tomatoes, two diced and one cut into wedges
1/2 cup canned black olives, sliced
2 avocados, sliced
4 hardboiled eggs, sliced
1 pkg. Mexican seasoned vegetarian ground meat substitute
1-2 cans chili-seasoned red beans
1/2 cup grated cheddar, Monterey Jack cheese, or soy cheese
1/4 cup sour cream (optional)
Salsa (any variety)
Balsamic dressing

Tear lettuce into pieces or cut into thin strips.

Warm beans in saucepan. Warm Mexican seasoned meat substitute. Cut into strips.

Toss lettuce, scallion, pepper, diced tomatoes, and olives in a bowl. Divide mixture onto individual plates. Place tomato wedges, avocado slices, hardboiled egg slices and meat substitute around edge of the salad. On top of the tossed lettuce and vegetable combination, place 1/4 – 1/2 cup warm beans. Sprinkle grated cheese on top of beans. Add a dollop of sour cream and salsa if desired.

Serve with tortilla chips, salsa on the side, and Balsamic dressing.

Note: This recipe can also be made with chicken for non-vegetarians.

~*~

An author of romantic suspense and contemporary romance novels, **Reggi Allder** likes nothing better than tales of love lost, then found, or stories of heroes and heroines who discover love and wonder if they'll live long enough to enjoy it. When not writing, she enjoys her family, books, movies, walks and chocolate. Titles include *Her Country Heart*, *Shattered Rules*, and *Money, Power and Poison*. Visit Reggi at www.reggiallder.com.

## Susan Breen's Eggs in a Tomato-Spinach Sauce

This tasty meal comes from Lucy Gellman, who has spent a lot of time in France and knows all sorts of intriguing and fast recipes.

Prep time: 5-10 min.
Cooking time: 10 min.
Serves 2

1 tsp. olive oil
2 sm. tomatoes, chopped
1-2 bags spinach
10-12 oz. jar pasta sauce
2-3 eggs
2 cloves garlic
1 onion, diced
4 hearty slices of baguette
Cheese (your choice of goat cheese, camembert, feta, Parmesan, Manchego, or mozzarella)
Black pepper, basil, sea salt, and cinnamon (optional)
Splash of wine (optional)

Because this recipe cooks rather quickly and needs supervision, prepare the bread beforehand. Just place 2 slices of bread on each plate and set the cheese aside.

In a medium-size saucepan, sauté onion and garlic and whatever spices you choose to use. Heat until garlic is slightly browned.

Add spinach to saucepan in two stages, allowing it to cook down. Stir in tomatoes, tomato sauce, and optional splash of wine and cinnamon or other spices. Reduce the heat, bringing the mixture to a slow boil.

Crack the eggs one at a time into the sauce, delicately enough so that they remain afloat. (If they sink, they will scramble a bit but still be delicious.) Using a teaspoon or spatula, gently baste the egg whites in the tomato liquid until they are firm, about 3 min. Cook 30 sec. – 1 min. more for runny yolks, longer for firmer yolks.

When finished, place on the bread, and sprinkle with cheese.

~*~

**Susan Breen** is the author of the novel, *The Fiction Class*. Her stories and articles have been published widely, most recently in *Best American Non-Required Reading*, *Ellery Queen Mystery Magazine*, and online at Queen Anne Bolyn. Her new mystery series, Maggie Dove, will be published next year. She lives with her family in Irvington, NY and she only cooks fast meals. Visit Susan at www.susanjbreen.com.

## Michelle Markey Butler's Simple but Splendid Medieval Feast

Prep time: 20 min., plus 1 hr. for bread to rise
Cooking time: 30-40 min.
Serves 10-12

Want to impress guests with a dish that looks much more difficult than it is, and makes them feel like they wandered into a fifteenth-century Great Hall?

3 lbs. frozen bread or roll dough
1/2 lb. hard cheese (Cheddar, Gouda, etc.,) grated
1 lb. smoked sausage or kielbasa, cut into 3" pieces
6 eggs, washed

Thaw bread dough. Preheat oven to 400 degrees.

Grease a large pizza pan. Using half the bread dough, make a circle of dough in the pizza pan about 1/3" thick and full width of the pan.

Pile the grated cheese in the center of the dough circle. Using a third of the remaining bread dough, make a smaller circle of dough and cover the cheese.

Place 5 of the eggs and the sausage sections around the cheese mound, alternating egg and sausage. Using the remaining bread dough, make ropes of dough and "tie" down the eggs and sausage. You can also create a decorative pattern on the top of the cheese mound.

Allow dough to rise 1 hr., then beat the remaining egg and brush the top of the bread with it.

Bake 15-20 min. (add 5 min. if you used a smaller pizza pan and the base dough is thicker,) then reduce heat to 350 degrees and bake another 15-

20 min.

To eat, peel the egg and eat separately or place it back into the bread and eat together.

~*~

**Michelle Markey Butler** is a lecturer at the University of Maryland. She teaches medieval literature, Tolkien, and Harry Potter. Her research focuses on web-based literary criticism and medieval to early modern drama. She's the author of a medieval-inspired historical fantasy novel, *Homegoing*. *The Last Abbot of Linn Duachaill*, written with co-author Jess Barry, is an upcoming historical novel about a Viking invasion in 9th century Ireland. Visit Michelle at www.michellemarkeybutler.com.

## Mariposa Cruz' Orient Express Main Course Coleslaw

Prep time: 15 min. (plus 30 min. to chill)
Serves 2

1 bag shredded coleslaw
1 can Mandarin oranges (in water or light syrup,) drained
1 can water chestnuts, drained and halved
1 bottle poppy seed salad dressing
Rice noodles or sliced almonds

Mix first three ingredients with dressing to desired consistency. Chill at least 30 min., then top with sliced almonds or crispy rice noodles and serve.

~*~

**Mariposa Cruz** balances writing with working as a fulltime corporate paralegal. As a writer, she's interviewed a variety of real-life characters from cowboy crooners to rock divas. Her articles have appeared in local magazines and indie newspapers. Her fiction titles include paranormal thrillers, *Howl* and *Roar* as well as contemporary romances, *Package Deal* and *Hot Flash*. She currently resides with her own pack of two kids in Reno, Nevada. Visit Mariposa at www.mariposacruz.blogspot.com.

## Conda V. Douglas' Quick and Easy Everyday Everything Sauce

This is my make-often-go-to basic sauce that goes well on almost everything, except perhaps ice cream. There are myriad uses for this sauce and tons of variations. The recipe may be doubled and freezes well.

Serving suggestions: Use as a soup base for creamy soups, as a cream sauce for beef stroganoff or over ground beef, poured over steamed veggies and spaghetti for a Pasta Primavera, or add curry to make a curry sauce and serve over rice with shrimp, chicken, pork, or beef and vegetables.

Prep time: 1 min.
Cooking time: 10 min.
Serves 4

1/4 cup flour (any variety, including gluten-free, except potato flour)
1/4 cup oil (olive, coconut, or canola)
1 cup broth (any variety)
1 cup full-fat milk (or soy, rice, almond or coconut milk)
4 heaping T. Brewer's yeast (optional)

Place the flour and any seasonings (see variations below) in a saucepan. Add in the broth and milk slowly, stirring continuously with a whisk until smooth.

Add oil. Heat on medium-high heat, stirring often until thickened. If too thick, add broth or milk. If too thin, whisk in a little more flour.

Variations: For a spicier sauce add onion powder, garlic powder, chili powder and black pepper to taste. For a Mexican-style sauce add a tablespoon each of cumin, coriander, chili powder (optional,) and cilantro.

~*~

**Conda V. Douglas** grew up in Sun Valley, Idaho. Her childhood, filled with artists, goats in the kitchen, buffalo bones in the living room, and rocks in the bathtub, is the inspiration for her tales (along with her odd family, including her bank robbing grandmother.) She's renamed Sun Valley as Starke in her Starke Dead mystery series and as Sprite in her Mall Fairies series. Visit Conda at condascreativecenter.blogspot.com.

## Mariana Gabrielle's Falafel with Cucumber Yogurt Sauce

Prep time: 30 min. (can be made ahead)
Cooking time: 30 min.
Serves 4-6

1 lb. uncooked garbanzo beans, soaked overnight and drained
1 bunch cilantro (stems okay)
1/2 sm. onion, diced
2 cloves garlic
1 sm. chili pepper, minced
1-2 T. coriander, to taste
1-2 T. cumin, to taste
1/4 – 1/2 tsp. cardamom, to taste (optional)
1 tsp. baking soda
1/2 tsp. salt, to taste
Canola oil

In a food processor, pulse beans and salt until they're the consistency of coarse sand. Add the rest of the ingredients and pulse, scraping down the sides with a spatula, until bright green, finely ground paste forms. It should be granular, not smooth. Refrigerate 20 min. to overnight.

Use a small scoop or tablespoon to form balls a bit smaller than a golf ball and flatten slightly. In a nonstick pan or cast iron skillet, heat 1/4" of canola oil on medium-high heat until it sizzles when a tiny bit of falafel is dropped in, then lower heat to medium.

Test with one falafel (kind of like pancakes, the first one probably won't be right.) Fry 5-7 min. until all sides are a deep golden brown. If it browns too quickly, turn the heat down a bit. If the falafels stick to the pan, you can lightly dredge them in a bit of flour.

Place in a warm oven until ready to use, up to 20 min.

Serve in pita bread, with yogurt sauce (recipe below) and sliced tomatoes, onions, and cucumber.

Note: Make two batches, form falafels, and freeze on a wax paper-covered cookie sheet. Store up to 3 months in an airtight freezer container, and only fry as much as you need for one meal at a time. (Add 3-4 min. to cooking time.)

## Cucumber Yogurt Sauce

10 oz. Greek yogurt
1 cucumber, shredded, with most of the juice pressed out (I press it lightly on a slotted spoon)
4-6 T. finely chopped fresh mint, dill, flat-leaf parsley, and/or cilantro, to taste
2-3 T. lemon juice, to taste
3-4 cloves garlic, minced
1 tsp. salt, to taste
Freshly ground pepper, to taste
Dash of ground cayenne or cayenne sauce, to taste (optional)

Mix all ingredients together. Let rest covered in refrigerator at least 1-2 hrs.

~*~

Regency romance author **Mariana Gabrielle** is not at all romantic, so she lives vicariously through her characters, who believe in their own happily-ever-afters. And believe they must, as they all suffer hearts bruised, broken, and scarred long before they reach her books. Mariana is also an editor and designer, and a member of the Bluestocking Belles and the Rocky Mountain Fiction Writers. Her books include *Royal Regard* and *La Déesse Noire: The Black Goddess*. Visit Mariana at www.marianagabrielle.com.

## Heather Hiestand's Dinner and Dessert Smoothie

When I'm really pressed for time, I like to make smoothies for dinner. Here's a simple, delicious recipe that's healthy but tastes like dessert. It contains enough calories to get you through the evening without overdoing it, despite the dessert-like flavor. Calories will vary depending, most especially, on the kind of milk you add.

Prep time: under 5 min.
Serves 1

2 frozen bananas
1 T. nut butter
1 scoop chocolate protein powder
1/4 tsp. cinnamon
1/4 tsp. vanilla extract
1 cup milk (dairy or non-dairy)
1 cup greens (spinach, romaine or kale)

Load ingredients into your blender and blend 30-60 seconds, depending on your blender's motor. Pour into a cup and enjoy.

~*~

Bestselling author **Heather Hiestand** writes the British-set Redcakes series, set in the 1880s/1890s around a teashop, and the Grand Russe series, set in the 1920s around a hotel. She's also the author of many novels, novellas, and short stories. Visit Heather at www.heatherhiestand.com.

## M.M. Jaye's Greek "All in One Pot" Cheese Pie

Preparation time: 10 min.
Cooking time: 40-50 min.
Serves 5

Nonstick cooking spray or butter
4 cups milk
5 oz. margarine
10 oz. feta cheese
3 eggs, whisked
1/4 tsp. nutmeg
4 sheets filo pastry
7 oz. Irish regato or other hard cheese (shredded)

Preheat oven at 350 degrees. Grease a rectangular 13" x 9" baking dish with nonstick cooking spray or butter.

Pour milk in medium-size saucepan. Add margarine and stir over medium-high heat until margarine melts. Remove pan from stove. Crumble feta cheese over pan. Add whisked eggs and nutmeg.

Shred the filo pastry sheets over pan. Stir well and pour in baking dish. Use a fork to even out the filo.

Sprinkle the shredded cheese over surface and bake 45-50 min. or until surface is golden.

~*~

**M.M. Jaye** loves the Greek sun and all things happily-ever-after. Her time spreads thin between raising a five-year old daughter with a vampiric sleep pattern, teaching translation to Greek young adults, and writing her own love stories set in Greece. *Fate Accompli* is her first contemporary romance. Visit M.M. at www.mmjayewrites.com.

## Kathy McIntosh's Risotto with Butternut Squash & Caramelized Onions

People often think risotto takes constant stirring and forever to make. Not so. This recipe is fast and easy and if your laptop is close enough, you might be able to write between additions of broth.

Prep time: 25 min.
Cooking time: 30 min.
Serves 4

1 butternut squash
1-2 onions or shallots (or mixed)
Sherry or butter
Small amount of sugar
1 cup Arborio rice
2 cans chicken broth or stock
1/4 cup sundried tomatoes, chopped (if in oil, rinse and drain first; if dried, rehydrate before chopping)
1 tsp. dried basil
1 tsp. dried marjoram
1 cup fresh kale or spinach (optional)
Parmesan-Reggiano cheese

Peel and cube squash. Parboil until almost tender. While squash is cooking, caramelize onions in small amount of sherry or butter and a little sugar.

Place rice in bottom of heavy saucepan on medium heat. Heat the broth in the microwave or another pan and ladle it into the pan with the rice in 1/2 cup increments. No need to stand and stir it constantly. Just stir occasionally until the broth is absorbed, then add the next ladle.

Add onions halfway through. Add basil, marjoram, tomatoes, squash, and optional kale or spinach with the last of the broth. Cook until thick and creamy.

Grate Parmesan-Reggiano cheese over risotto before serving.

~*~

**Kathy McIntosh** is a recent transplant from Idaho to Arizona's Sonora desert. Her Havoc in Hancock humorous suspense novels set in Idaho include *Mustard's Last Stand* and *Foul Wind*. Her next book will be set amongst the saguaros. In addition to creating offbeat humorous suspense, Kathy writes and speaks about words and writing. When not learning about her new home or curled up reading, she loves to travel and explore different cultures and cuisines. Visit Kathy at www.kathymcintosh.com.

## Claire A. Murray's Black Beans and Brown Rice Casserole

This dish creates a fully satisfying meal, but it can also be served cold as an appetizer with tortilla chips or pita bread if you cut the vegetables small enough.

Prep time: 5-10 min.
Cooking time: 10 min.
Serves 4-6

1 cup instant brown rice
28 oz. canned peeled or crushed tomatoes
14 oz. can black beans
1 lg. zucchini
1 yellow squash (optional)
1 med. onion
1 lg. green or red pepper
1-2 heaping T. garlic in oil
2 heaping T. spicy mustard (seeded preferable)
Small amount of cooking oil
Salt and pepper, to taste

Chop all vegetable into bite size chunks or manageable strips for easy eating.

Sauté vegetables in small amount of oil in large frying pan or sauté pan until onion is translucent. Stir in tomatoes, black beans (including liquid,) and garlic.

Bring to a low boil and add rice. Add any other seasonings you wish. Lower the cooking temperature to simmer. Cover and let simmer 5 min. Turn off burner and let stand 10-15 min. before serving.

~*~

Mystery author **Claire A. Murray** has published several short stories, including *Tug-of-War, Mother's Mountain, The Drop, Miss Aggie's Pigs,* and *Cheating Death*. She's currently working on her second novel while revising her first novel. Visit Claire at www.facebook.com/Clairemurraywrites.

## Ann Myers' Southwest-style Eggs in Purgatory

I love the name of this dish of eggs suspended in a bubbling tomato sauce. It's also quick, inexpensive, and flexible. Classic recipes use Italian or Middle Eastern herbs and spices, but here the fire comes from Southwest chili.

Prep time: 10 min.
Cooking time: 25–35 min.
Serves: 4

1 T. olive oil
1 sm. onion, diced (about 2/3 cup)
1 clove garlic, minced
1-2 tsp. chili powder, to taste
1 tsp. ground cumin
1/2 tsp. ground coriander
1/2 tsp. dried oregano
1/4 – 1/2 tsp. salt, to taste
Ground black pepper, to taste
Red pepper flakes (optional)
2/3 cup water or broth, divided
28 oz. canned diced tomatoes (or an approximate equivalent amount fresh tomatoes, whirled in a food processor until saucy but still chunky)
4 eggs
1/2 cup grated cheddar, Monterey Jack, fresh farmer's or Mexican cheese
Corn or flour tortillas, crusty bread, fluffy *sopapillas*, or rice
Optional garnishes: sour cream, Mexican *crema*, chopped cilantro and/or chives, diced avocado dressed in lime juice, and salt.

Heat oil in lg. skillet or sauté pan over medium heat. Add onions, stirring frequently until onions are soft and translucent.
Mix in minced garlic, cumin, coriander, and red chili. Stir 1-2 min. Add

tomatoes, 1/3 cup water or broth, oregano, salt, and pepper. Simmer gently about 15 min.

Taste for seasoning and check that the mixture is still somewhat soupy (add the extra water or broth if it seems dry.) Create little wells for the eggs in the tomato mixture. Crack an egg into each well. If you're concerned about stray shells, crack each egg into a bowl and pour from there into the tomato mixture. Cover and cook eggs 5-7 min. or more, depending on how you like your eggs. Check occasionally, jiggling the pan so that the eggs don't stick to the bottom. Sunny or medium-side up works well in this recipe because the eggs will cook more when broken into the hot tomatoes.

When eggs are nearly done, uncover and sprinkle with cheese, aiming for the tomato and egg whites rather than the yolks. Let the cheese melt 1-2 min. Serve immediately in wide pasta or soup bowls, garnished with the optional toppings and a side of seasoned pinto beans or green salad.

~*~

**Ann Myers** loves cooking, crafts, and cozy mysteries. Her debut culinary cozy, *Bread of the Dead*, is set in Santa Fe, New Mexico and features café chef and amateur sleuth Rita Lafitte. Rita and her friends return in the second book of the series, *Cinco de Mayhem*, along with recipes for a Cinco de Mayo feast. Visit Ann at www.facebook.com/AnnMyers.writer.

## Kathryn Quick's Mexican Tortilla Casserole

Prep time: 5 min.
Cooking time: approximately 30 min.
Serves 4

Nonstick cooking spray
1 T. olive oil
1 onion, chopped
1 tsp. ground cumin
1-1/2 tsp. chili powder
1 tsp. minced garlic
14 oz. can chopped tomatoes, drained (reserve 1/2 cup juice)
1/2 cup tomato paste
31 oz. canned beans (your choice kidney, black, white beans or combination,) rinsed and drained
5 oz. can sweet kernel corn, drained (or 1/2 cup frozen corn, thawed)
3 cups spinach, coarsely chopped
4 med. 8" tortillas
2 cups Monterey Jack cheese, shredded
Salt and pepper, to taste
Cilantro (optional)
Sour cream
Salsa

Option: add cooked chicken or beef to the bean mixture and reduce the amount of beans to 1 can.

Preheat oven to 400 degrees.

Spray 9" round cake pan or baking dish with nonstick spray.

Heat oil in a large skillet over medium heat. Add onion, cumin, chili powder and garlic, cooking until the onion is soft and you can smell the spices. Add tomatoes with some on the reserved juice, tomato paste and beans. Simmer 3 min. Add corn and spinach. Simmer until spinach is wilted. Salt and pepper to taste.

Place 1 tortilla in prepared pan. Spread one-quarter of the mixture and sprinkle with 1/2 cup of shredded cheese. Repeat for 3 more layers ending with cheese.

Bake about 20 min. until top is slightly browned. Let stand 5 min., then cut into wedges. Sprinkle top with cilantro if desired and serve with sour cream and salsa.

Tip: You can make this ahead and refrigerate. When ready to cook, let stand at room temperature about 20 min. You can also reheat cooked casserole at 350 degrees for 15-20 min.

~*~

**Kathryn Quick** writes contemporary romances, romantic comedy, and historical romances. She also writes urban fantasy as P.K. Eden with writing partner Patt Mihailoff.

Current releases include *Ineligible Bachelor* and *Bachelor-Dot-Com*, the first two books in her Bachelors Three series, loosely based on reality TV and popular among those enjoying a "chick-flick" type read.

In her "other" life, Kathryn works in county government in New Jersey and is married with three sons. Visit Kathryn at www.kathrynquick.com.

## Terry Shames' Arugula Main Course Salad

In July 2015, surgery on my shoulder resulted in a complication that had a big impact on my writing and cooking: during the surgery my radial nerve was damaged in my right (dominant) hand. It meant that I would have limited use of my right hand for many months. As for writing, my left hand stepped up in a major way, so typing, although slower, was possible. Also, I could use Dragon to "write" orally. Unfortunately, Dragon doesn't work for cooking. And although my husband is a smart man of many talents, in the kitchen he's like a newborn.

Chopping ingredients is very difficult with one hand. I could do a little, but it took time and effort—time I'd rather spend writing. So I developed recipes that called for little or no kitchen skills. The following is a healthful salad that can be a light dinner, or with the addition of pretty much any meat, chicken, or seafood, works as a hearty meal.

4 cups baby arugula
1/2 cup toasted walnuts
1/2 cup feta cheese, crumbled
1 cup seedless red grapes
2 T. lemon juice
4 T. olive oil (good quality)
Salt and pepper, to taste
1 tsp. fresh herbs such as basil, oregano, or thyme (optional)

Combine first four ingredients in a bowl.

Whisk together lemon juice, olive oil, salt and pepper, and optional herbs.

Drizzle over salad and toss.
Variations: Instead of grapes, use dried cranberries (1/2 cup), sliced

pear, peach, or apple. Use pecans instead of walnuts. Substitute blue cheese or goat cheese for feta. For a heartier dish, add shrimp or chicken.

~*~

**Terry Shames** writes the bestselling Samuel Craddock series. *A Killing at Cotton Hill* won the Macavity Award for Best First Mystery of 2013. *The Last Death of Jack Harbin* was a finalist for a Macavity Award for Best Mystery, 2014. *A Deadly Affair at Bobtail Ridge* launched in April, 2015. *The Necessary Death of Nonie Blake*, comes out in January, 2016. Visit Terry at www.terryshames.com.

# Timesaving Tips

# Cooking Tips

Good tools can save you time. I love my apple corer. With one push it gets rid of the core and makes 8 perfect slices. —Ashlyn Chase

~*~

For recipes that require browned hamburger meat, you can save time in the kitchen by frying up 5-10 lb. of meat at a time. Pat the hamburger dry with paper towels to remove excess grease. Divide into 1 lb. portions and place in plastic sandwich bags. Place the sandwich bags into a one-gallon freezer bag and freeze. —Sandra McGregor

~*~

For one-dish dinners that freeze well, such as lasagna, double the recipe and freeze one for a night when you're too busy to do anything other than pop a dish in the oven to heat up. —Judy Penz Sheluk

~*~

Don't toss out raw vegetables that are beginning to look a little "sad." Use them in pasta dishes, stews, and soups. —Judy Penz Sheluk

~*~

Plan a week's worth of dinner menus ahead of time and shop for all the ingredients in one trip. This avoids multiple trips to the supermarket during the week. —Kaye Spencer

~*~

Buy a rice maker. They're easy to use, and they keep your rice warm so it's ready when you are. I also make quinoa and packaged noodles in mine. —Joanna Campbell Slan

~*~

On a monthly basis, I make a list of ten dinner recipes and locate or purchase all the non-perishable ingredients. I buy the perishable ingredients on a weekly basis, knowing that I have the rest of the ingredients on hand. —Margaret S. Hamilton

~*~

I keep my spices in alphabetical order. This avoids having to waste time hunting for the right one. —L.C. Hayden

~*~

Whenever I'm in the kitchen, I plan to make at least two or three meals at a time. During dinner I'll cut up veggies for tomorrow's omelet, or prep overnight oatmeal for the fridge. If I'm making lunch, I'll precook rice for dinner or marinate some meat. —Cori Lynn Arnold

~*~

A little prepping ahead saves hours in the kitchen over the course of a week. You've heard the term "plan ahead"? In my family we Prep Ahead. My husband and I both work full time, and being a published author is my second job. This is how we get dinner on the table in thirty minutes every night. We search grocery store flyers for sales on chicken. When it comes down to $1/lb., we buy twenty-five chicken breasts on the bone. (Having a second freezer in the garage helps with storage.) The day we're going to have grilled or roasted chicken for dinner, we cook up four servings per person. Now we've got cooked chicken for the entire week. —Ava Bradley

~*~

Save leftover bits of meats and vegetables throughout the week for a weekend soup pot. Add broth, canned tomatoes, noodles, or whatever is needed to create the right consistency. —Judy Alter

~*~

Always keep easy-to-make food in your freezer: burritos, potpies, pirogies, hot dogs and burgers. That way, when you've once again forgotten to defrost that roast or chicken, you can whip up a quick meal. Cook a healthy meal with lots of vegetables at least three times a week to redeem yourself. —Irene Peterson

~*~

Teach your kids to cook. —Irene Peterson

~*~

Chopping onions always bother my eyes, so when I have to chop onions for a recipe, I double the amount and store half in a zip-top plastic bag or plastic food container. This saves me time plus an episode of tears for the next meal where I need a chopped onion, a staple of the holy trinity in cooking. —Marni Graff

~*~

This is a great way to use up fruit languishing in your fruit bowl. Make a big bowl of fruit-filled Jell-o once a week. I chop apples (any and all sorts,) oranges, bananas, peaches, blueberries and plums and drop in some pomegranate seeds, cherries, and any other fruits on hand. Any Jell-o flavor works. Stir in one or two scoops of applesauce. You can also add coconut flakes, dried cranberries, almond slices, raisins, flaxseeds or oatmeal flakes. This makes a fast, delicious and relatively nutritious breakfast. Scoop some into a bowl and add a dollop of your favorite yogurt on top. An added bonus: you save fruit from rotting and ending up in the compost pile or garbage. —Gemma Juliana

~*~

I do a lot of holiday baking. To save time I make up my own dry mixes the first time I bake. While I have all the ingredients out, I fill zip-top plastic bags with the dry ingredients. This makes baking subsequent batches easier. I just assemble the wet ingredients and add my pre-measured dry ingredients. —Linda Gordon Hengerer

~*~

I make double batches of cookie dough, put them in a plastic container, and chill the dough. Having a container of cookie dough lets me bake as much or as little as I need at any time. —Linda Gordon Hengerer
Instead of greasing cookie sheets, I use parchment paper. This saves cleanup time and makes it easier and faster to move the cookies from the cookie sheet to the cooling rack. I hold the long edge of the parchment paper with one hand, the baking sheet in the other hand, and while I tilt the baking sheet, I pull the parchment paper onto the cooling rack. —Linda Gordon Hengerer

~*~

When time is tight, it can be worth buying pre-made meals. However, often the canned, boxed, or frozen meals are unhealthy and expensive. Mix in vegetables to make them healthier and increase the number of servings. Add frozen broccoli to powdered broccoli cheese soup. Add a bag of fresh or frozen stir-fry veggies to a stir-fry mix. Stir a bag of fresh spinach into boxed pasta. Salsa is a tasty addition to macaroni and cheese. This helps reduce the guilt of using prepared meals. —Kris Bock

~*~

Freeze in-season berries spread out on cookie sheets, then store in freezer bags. Blanch green vegetables a few minutes, then freeze the same way. You can also do this with sliced fruits, but sprinkle with a bit of ascorbic acid to inhibit browning. —Mariana Gabrielle

~*~

Work a recipe backwards—if the recipe calls for items to be added in groups or steps, I work backwards and assemble the ingredients in one bowl or cup. For instance if the last three ingredients are butter, salt and seasoning, I put those in one bowl at the end of the line, then work the line to the beginning of the recipe. When it's time to cook, all the measuring is done and I just add the bowls of ingredients successively. —Jayne Ormerod

~*~

Don't throw the bones away. Before I roast chicken, I bone it and keep the rib cage and back. It makes delicious chicken soup and extra dinners. —M.M. Jaye

~*~

When I need a dessert, I bake one-bowl cakes, then sprinkle them with powdered sugar instead of making icing. —Karen Rose Smith

~*~

I always keep on hand a dozen eggs, canned tuna, and canned chicken. These foods can be added to frozen food packages to make them more enticing and nutritious. —Kay Kendall

~*~

Get your husband to do the grocery shopping and cook dinner. —Lea Wait

~*~

Instead of peeling fresh ginger root, which is time-consuming, try this trick: Stick the ginger root in a plastic bag and place it in the freezer.

Whenever you need some, use a cheese grater to grate it, skin and all. You won't be able to tell the difference. —Elizabeth Rose

~*~

Pressed for time in the morning? Do the prep work for your slow cooker meals the night before. Store in the refrigerator. In the morning, simple pop the cooker insert into the cooker and turn on. —Lisa Alber

~*~

You can boil water faster in an electric kettle than on the stove. To cut down on the time it takes to make pasta, heat water in an electric kettle and pour it into the pasta pot. If you need more water, add tap water to the pot or fill the electric kettle again to boil additional water. Either way, the water will be ready for the pasta quicker than if you started with cold water from the tap. —Maya Corrigan

~*~

Chose recipes that don't rely heavily on measurements. It saves time by not having to clean extra measuring cups, spoons, bowls, etc. and meals are quickly prepared. —Claudia Lefeve

~*~

Cook with friends. Gather a couple of friends together on a Saturday and prepare a week's worth of freezable dinners. When the muse is humming, all you have to do is thaw one out and pop it in the oven. —Lynn Kinnaman

# Household Tips

Buy a Rumba robot floor cleaner. It automatically starts to work at a preset time and turns itself off when finished. It does a great job on my hardwood floors. —Sandra McGregor

~*~

When ironing, only iron the front of T-shirts, shirts and blouses. After all, that's all people can see. —Marie Laval

~*~

Sitting too long at a computer is bad for your health. Schedule breaks to get up and move, but make that time do double-duty by tackling a household chore, such as laundry or vacuuming, during each break. —Kaye Spencer

~*~

I keep a master list on the kitchen bulletin board with everything I buy at a big box store (paper goods, cleaning supplies, canned goods, pantry staples.) Once a month, I stock up. —Margaret S. Hamilton

~*~

I tie colorful ribbons from gifts I've received around sheet sets so individual pieces don't stray. That way, I never have to waste time hunting for matching pillowcases and sheets. — L.C. Hayden

~*~

Cleaning the bathroom is one of my least favorite chores, so I'm always looking for ways to make it easier. Plus, having to use bleach and other harsh chemicals on the shower tiles to keep mold and mildew down is not the healthiest or most environmentally-friendly way to go. So we use a microfiber bath towel to wipe down the shower area after use. It wicks the moisture away, helps prevent growth of the scuzzies, and saves hours of scrubbing. —B.V. Lawson

~*~

I think in our Pinterest-perfect, magazine-photoshopped world, it's often easy to think we have to be perfect when it comes to housekeeping. Who says sock and underwear drawers have to be neat? Or that a little bit of clutter is a sin? In setting my life priorities, I've decided that writing and sharing life with family and friends are far more important than being OCD about a clean house. After all, how many of us will lie on our deathbeds one day and say, "My only regret is that I didn't dust more."? —B.V. Lawson

~*~

Iron shirts when they're still damp from the dryer, then let them dry on hangers. This saves dryer time and the steam created by this process makes the shirts look great. —Gemma Juliana

~*~

In my busy family, schedules rule everything—sports, music, school—so I applied a schedule to our household chores. Laundry is done on Fridays and Saturdays. Bathrooms are cleaned on Mondays. We dust on Wednesdays, vacuum and mop on Thursdays. —Renée Reynolds

~*~

Play music while doing chores—preferably hard rock. I swear it saves time because you're focusing on the music instead of grimacing and whining while washing dishes or dusting. And if you play music while mopping, sweeping or vacuuming, you naturally want to dance, so you get exercise! Do this often and you'll have a clean house and a skinny waistline. (And you really do work faster with music.) —Flo Fitzpatrick

~*~

Place a handful of empty trash bags in the bottom of your wastepaper basket. When you remove the full bag, you have a new one handy. —Mariana Gabrielle

~*~

When cooking, I fill my sink with hot, soapy water. As I finish with a utensil or bowl, I drop it in the sink. When clean-up time comes, everything is basically washed. —Jayne Ormerod

~*~

Hire a maid! —Jayne Ormerod

~*~

Place a sheet of tin foil on the bottom of the oven. When the foil is dirty, discard and replace. —Helena Fairfax

~*~

Heat a cupful of water in the microwave before cleaning. The steam will loosen any dried-on dirt. —Helena Fairfax

~*~

I clean my stainless steel with white vinegar. It works well and costs much less than stainless steel cleaner. —Sandra Masters

~*~

We keep antibacterial wipes stored in each bathroom. Every Saturday morning, there's no television/video games/fun allowed until each child wipes down his bathroom. By having the wipes in the bathroom, no one can complain they can't find what they need to do the job. —Melinda Curtis

~*~

You don't need to sort your silverware after taking it out of the dishwasher. You may occasionally find yourself eating cereal with a fork, but you'll also save yourself 5-15 minutes a day. —Susan Breen

~*~

Pairing up socks after doing the laundry was annoying and time-consuming, and there was always that one sock that was missing a mate. I bought 18 pairs of exactly the same white ankle socks and threw out all the rest. Now it takes only seconds to put them away. —Lida Bushloper

~*~

Lightly spray water on a microfiber cloth before dusting. You'll trap more dust in the cloth. —Kathy McIntosh

# Organizational Tips

For me, the key to juggling everything I do is goal setting. I created a wall quilt to remind me of my goals. I printed out my goals, laminated them, and attached a piece of self-adhesive Velcro to the back of each. I sewed another piece of Velcro to the center of the quilt squares. My goal quilt is a constant reminder of not just where I am going but how far I've come—an inspiration on even the toughest of days or weeks. If you don't sew, a simple alternative is a photo board, available at most craft and home goods stores. —Tara Neale

~*~

I'm a list maker. If I have to run errands, I list every place in driving order with a note of what I need at each location. That way I don't forget one of the stops. I also always make a shopping list and have a pad of paper and pen in the kitchen to write down what we need when something is used up. I've even trained the hubby to write things down. —Pepper Phillips

~*~

I keep a travel toiletries inventory on a file card in my travel bag. After a trip, I replace with fresh supplies. I also have a short inventory list to review when I check out of a hotel: phone and camera chargers, computer cords, and the nightie hanging on the bathroom door. —Margaret S. Hamilton

~*~

Implement an occasional Catch-Up Day. When you feel overwhelmed, plan a day or two where you catch up on e-mails, phone calls, and the endless list of tasks you've been putting off. You can also use that day to schedule your to-do list and calendar so that you won't get so overwhelmed again. —Stacy Juba

~*~

Use three-tiered wire kitchen baskets in other parts of the house. Hang them from the ceiling in a closet for extra storage. It's a great spot for swimwear, socks, and underwear. Hang them in your office to hold scissors, staplers, and art supplies. Hang them in the playroom to hold stuffed animals and toys. —L.C. Hayden

~*~

To avoid spending time untangling necklace chains, attach decorative thumb tacks to a closet wall and drape necklaces from them. —L.C. Hayden

~*~

Grouping medicines by category makes it easier to find what you're looking for in the medicine cabinet whenever you have a headache or a bug bite. Place each group in zip-top plastic bags. —L.C. Hayden

~*~

When my husband and I downsized from a spacious house into a condo of less than 1,000 square feet, I went from having a large walk-in closet to a small apartment-sized closet. I needed to downsize my expansive wardrobe. Having fewer items makes it easier to dress in the morning and makes it easier to find ways to mix and match. It forces me to buy only clothes that I love and that fit well, not that *might* fit after I lose those excess pounds. I also don't waste time standing in front of the closet each morning, wondering what to wear. —Lourdes Venard

~*~

Do all of your keys look alike? Use a different color nail polish to paint the top of each key a different color. No more trying several keys before finding the right one. —Cynthia Luhrs

~*~

Lots of cupcake liners cluttering up your shelves? Stack them all together in a wide mouth Mason jar. Personally, I think Mason jars are fantastic for organizing all kinds of things. —Cynthia Luhrs

~*~

Use a Note app to keep your grocery list on your phone instead of writing lists on paper. Add items as you run out, and keep a section of frequently used items such as salad greens, milk and bread. You might forget a paper list, but you always have your phone. —Cynthia Luhrs

~*~

Clean and organize your desk at night and plan the next day's work. —Judy Alter

~*~

I keep a jacketed folder for each of my three son's families and toss in my copies of programs from recitals, ticket stubs, newspaper articles—any of their mementos or special events for the entire family. When it comes time for a birthday or holiday gift, a small scrapbook of someone's big moments will make that gift card tucked inside seem like so much more. —Marni Graff

~*~

Don't dump your mail on the counter! I grew up in a house where one kitchen counter was always covered with mail. After marrying and having a family of my own, I discovered one of the easiest ways to control clutter is to sort mail immediately. Pay what needs paying, file what needs filing, and recycle what you don't want to see again. —

Renée Reynolds

~*~

Have a place for everything. When finished using an item, put it back where it belongs. —Sharleen Scott

~*~

Hang your clothes in "outfits" so you can grab and go in the morning. —Kathryn Quick

~*~

Hang your keys on your purse with a carabineer clip so you never have to search for them. —Kathryn Quick

~*~

Instead of recycling glass food jars, I save them. They've become a real timesaver in the kitchen. When I open a bag of rice or a box of pasta and don't use the entire contents, I place the leftover in a glass jar. There's no need to label because I can instantly see what's inside. For food products that look alike, I take a black marker and write on the jars. Similar items are stored together, so when I'm going grocery shopping, a quick glance at the jars tells me what I need. —Elizabeth John

~*~

Here's another tip for glass jars: After I've painted a room in my house, I pour the leftover paint into a glass jar and label it with the color, brand, and type. I store the jar in a closet in the room I painted. If a wall needs retouching, I have the original paint handy. No searching through piles of rusty paint cans or racking my brain trying to remember the color. —Elizabeth John

~*~

Tote bags are wonderful tools for saving time. I designate specific ones for different areas of my life and stuff them accordingly to grab and go at a moment's notice. I keep an unopened water bottle in each bag and hang them on heavy-duty hangers in the hall closet. —Elizabeth John

~*~

We have different baskets in the house for different types of laundry. There's one for whites, one for sports uniforms and practice clothes, one for delicates, etc. This reduces sorting time and allows me to look at the baskets and manage which type of laundry has priority. —Melinda Curtis

~*~

I hate clutter and running out of necessities. In my house each child has a small basket for the things needed to get ready in the morning (toothbrush, hair care products, etc.) This keeps all items contained, and I can tell at a glance if anything needs restocking. —Melinda Curtis

~*~

File anything needed for taxes in an appropriate folder as soon as you receive it. Keep receipts! Having everything in one place makes filling out tax forms quicker and easier. —Lea Wait

~*~

Do you constantly waste time searching for where you left your keys or your glasses? Designate a specific place for each and always keep them there. —Lynn Kinnaman

# Writing Tips

Maintain a database and calendar for each book. In the database record each character's name, age, occupation, physical appearance, and relationship to the other characters. When you add something about the character in your story, such as where she went to college or the name of a childhood pet, add the information to the database. This is especially handy when writing an ongoing series as it keeps you from making mistakes in future books. The calendar is used to record on which days the scenes in your book take place. Pick a starting date for your story, then record scenes as the story unfolds. This allows you to keep track of the time that has elapsed in your story and avoids timeline errors. —Lois Winston

~*~

I *love* research and save links I discover for reference. If you're like me, after a while you have a Favorites folder so large it's impossible to navigate. I discovered a Microsoft product called *One Note*. I use it for organizing my writing research, but you can use it to organize anything. —Rose Anderson

~*~

Schedule a set time of day and amount of time to check your social media accounts. Treating social media as an "appointment" vs. something that distracts you from writing will free up far more time than you can imagine. I typically schedule one hour a day for this. I also pre-schedule my Facebook posts, and often have 5-10 posts lined up. —Judy Penz Sheluk

~*~

Participate in National Novel Writing Month (NaNoWriMo) in November to complete the rough draft of a 50,000 word novel in thirty days. —Kaye Spencer

~*~

My organizational tip is…wait for it…—outline! I work full time and make dinner when I get home. Between work, dinner, cleanup, laundry, and the 1,073 other things women do every day, my massively detailed outlines keep my writing time creative and efficient. No grasping for plot points. No wondering when my sleuth is supposed to find the essential clue. My outlines are organic, changing when my characters take the story into their own hands. But with a detailed base, I can usually keep right up with them. —Alice Loweecey

~*~

Once, I asked poet Lucille Clifton, who had six children, how she found time to write. She told me she wrote in her head while she was doing her chores, trying out lines of her poetry over and over until she got them right. I've done that with dialogue, working on phrasing over and over in my head while I do chores or work out. —Laurel Peterson

~*~

Keep the momentum. When writing, if you come upon a fact to research or a stumbling block, put XXX where the problem is and keep writing. At the end of the day, you can go back and figure out what to replace your Xs with. —Joanna Campbell Slan

~*~

I use a timer for writing sprints, generally about twenty-five minutes. When the timer goes off, I save my work, get up, and clean house, cook, or give myself a break and visit the Internet. I also limit my time on the Internet the same way so I don't waste writing time. —Pepper Phillips

~*~

Limit the time you spend reading and dissecting reviews. I'm constantly amazed at how much time and energy writers spend agonizing over reviews they've received on social media. They grumble and express outrage, huddle with friends (virtually, if not in person) and wring their hands over why someone posted such cruel words. The time spent doing this is time you could be writing. If you absolutely can't resist the drama, set yourself a time limit, set a timer, and go for it. But once the timer goes off, get back to work. —Terry Shames

~*~

To avoid distractions while writing, remove your landline and/or cell phone from your writing area. Let the calls go to voicemail, and call back later when you've finished writing for the day. —Beverley Bateman

~*~

Writers, as well as many other people, spend a lot of time sitting while working. Exercise seems to be the one thing that gets pushed aside when deadlines loom. I combine my exercise with my writing for a two-for-one deal. Instead of sitting on a desk chair, I sit on an exercise ball. The ball allows me to exercise my core and leg muscles while working. Another option is to stand. I use my kitchen island for writing. I can stand at the counter and move my legs while I type. This gives me the needed break from sitting. —Melissa Keir

~*~

Create a laptop stand for your treadmill and write while walking. Or make a dent in your TBR pile by reading while you walk on the treadmill. —Melissa Keir

~*~

Get out of the house and walk when you're stuck with a plot point. I take my phone with me and use it to record ideas and notes while I walk. —Melissa Keir

~*~

I spend many hours a day on the computer. When I heard about treadmill desks I knew it was the perfect solution to combine exercise and writing. I found an inexpensive desk I could place on my current treadmill. Now I not only use it for writing but many other computer activities while walking for an hour or two daily. —Josie Riviera

~*~

Learn how to say "no." No one person can do it all. If writing is important to you, then make it a priority. Put it near the top of your list, just below husband, family, and job. Be realistic about when you write best and set aside that time to write. Accept that there will be interruptions you can't control, but be as serious about your writing time as you are about getting to work on time. —Skye Taylor

~*~

Write down your goal for each writing session—a word count, fixing a difficult scene, plotting the next chapter, editing a chapter, etc. Check the task off when you finish, and you'll feel the satisfaction of having accomplished your goal. —Skye Taylor

~*~

When I transitioned from a full-time office employee to a full-time freelancer, I found it hard to concentrate. I had plenty of work, but it was too easy to stop to do laundry, run errands, and log on to Facebook. I finally found a way to focus through the simple use of a free, web-based timer. I can set the timer for each project I'm working. At the end of the week, I receive a report of how much time I've spent and where I've spent it, including areas such as marketing and finding new clients. Using the timer forces me to sit and work. My goal is forty hours a week, just like an office job. I easily meet my goal these days, and my time is spent more productively. —Lourdes Venard

~*~

Create a list of words or phrases that you over-use on a regular basis. Use this list as a quick search tool during the editing phase of your writing. —C.A. Rowland

~*~

Don't keep re-writing the first chapter. It may turn out your story doesn't even start there. —Susan C. Shea

~*~

I'm a huge list maker. So every night before going to bed, I make a list of tasks I want to accomplish the next day, everything from "mop the floor" to "pay the phone bill," and I give them a priority ranking (high, medium, low.) I also add my writing goals for the day, such as "write 2,500 words on (work in progress) novel" or "outline book 4 in the Scott Drayco series." Then I prioritize the list, making sure that writing is toward the top, and I don't get sidetracked by the low-priority jobs. —B.V. Lawson

~*~

I'm a blogger. I set aside one day to write four or five blog posts and pre-schedule them. This saves time, and I don't have to stop when I've got a deadline or I'm in the flow of writing. —Linda Gordon Hengerer

~*~

When I start a book, I give myself a rough word count. I prepare an Excel spreadsheet and set a goal of 500 words a day. I then mark off the days of the months and back into when I will have the book finished. Then I subtract weekends, holidays, vacations, and the odd day off, and it stretches out to a more realistic writing schedule. When I write more than 500 words a day, I can take a longer weekend, an extra day off, or beat the schedule to finish the book. It's a goal oriented progress chart with a little self-discipline thrown in. —R. Franklin James

~*~

Take the time to explore the "options" or settings in your word processing program. You may discover some ways to simplify or streamline your writing and editing. —Kris Bock

~*~

When I'm writing and unsure of something or know I'll be going back to work on a section, I either highlight it or change the font to a different color. That way the section stands out as I scroll through to find it again. —Sandra Masters

~*~

When you begin a new novel, create a character list (a table works best.) Make columns for first name, last name and comments. Enter the characters' names as you write them into the novel. This will keep you from ending up with similar sounding names for your characters. —Judith Copek

~*~

Invest in Caller-ID for your landline. I never answer the phone unless I recognize the number. This avoids dealing with sales calls and robocalls. If the call is important, the caller will leave a message, and I'll return the call when I've finished writing for the day. —Lois Winston

~*~

On weekends, I like to visit open houses. For some reason, this activity stimulates my creativity. If I'm stumped by a plotting issue, all is resolved by the time I drive home. It's also a great way to promote my books. I always carry bookmarks with me and manage to work into the conversation that I'm an author. Realtors spend long afternoons at open houses and are often looking for a quick read. Plus, they have access to a huge database. If they like your books, they'll spread the word to everyone they know. —Cindy Sample

~*~

I used to spend way too much time jotting notes and scene ideas on Post Its and index cards, only to misplace them or have to pick through them all the time. I'd also expend more valuable time creating elaborate Excel spreadsheets to track my point of view characters. Then along came Scrivener, a software program for writers. Scrivener allows me to streamline my process, which provides me with more time for the actual writing. —Lisa Alber

~*~

As a short story writer, I find it helpful to keep a chart with deadlines and submission information. I include a column where I note if the story is accepted or rejected. I also list places to submit rejected stories, to keep them in circulation. I intend to add a column for rights acquired, so I know when I can send accepted stories out for reprints. —Paula Gail Benson

~*~

I keep a digital recorder in the car to record story ideas, flesh out a scene that's on my mind, or take note of things that are easy to omit from a story, especially sensory descriptions of things I pass along the way, such as the smell of the air in a densely wooded area after a brief rain or the sight of cardinal flying past my windshield. —Claire A. Murray

~*~

Plan your next scene in your head before you sit down to write. That way you don't waste precious writing time wondering what your characters should be doing next. —Ann Myers

~*~

Keep a notebook on your night table to jot down any inspirations that come to you in the middle of the night. Knowing that you won't forget your brilliant idea by morning makes it easier to fall asleep. —Maya Corrigan

~*~

I have a tough time getting started writing, particularly if it's been a few days since I last worked on a project. So I bribe myself with various television shows that are my guilty pleasures. If I write 100 words, I get to watch 5 minutes of *True Blood* or *Game of Thrones*. As I get going for the day, I adjust the word count to require more words for the treat. At some point I get into my story enough to abandon the TV show. But when I'm doing something difficult—like editing, or writing a scene that's not going well—the TV carrot helps me keep going. —Michelle Markey Butler

## Miscellaneous Tips

I listen to books on tape in the car instead of listening to music. It not only makes a long trip seem shorter, it makes a huge dent in my to-be-read pile. —Pepper Phillips

~*~

I save a lot of time by following my motto, "If it isn't worth complaining about, let it go." I don't mean I'm a bliss ninny—I do get upset about things. I allow myself the pleasure of a rant for a minute or two, or maybe a post on social media, but then I remember whose time I'm eating into by spending time and energy on the rant. I know people who seem to take umbrage at every little thing and spend enormous amounts of time and energy yelling about their latest outrage. If that works for them, fine. But time is precious, and ranting just to hear myself rant doesn't make sense in my life. —Terry Shames

~*~

Meditate. Studies show that meditation techniques can promote creative thinking, even if you have never meditated before. Spending 10 minutes meditating can clear your head enough to significantly increase your productivity. It also improves attention and concentration, helps to quiet your inner critic, makes you less vulnerable to the criticism of others, increases self-confidence, and reduces anxiety. You can find free downloadable meditations on the Internet or meditation apps for your phone or tablet. —Stacy Juba

~*~

My most important timesaving tip: take an afternoon nap if you can. It pays off in productivity later in the day. —Judy Alter

~*~

Do the grocery shopping as early in the morning as your store allows. No lines, so no wasting time reading headlines of tabloids while trying to avoid the candy. Plenty of parking spaces so you don't have to circle the lot. Also, memorize which aisles carry what you normally buy. Good for the brain and you don't waste time wandering around looking for the ingredients for Easy Texas Chili. —Flo Fitzpatrick

~*~

Purchase small gift items such as wine stoppers, notepads, non-perishable foods, etc. whenever you find them on sale and keep them in a basket or bin in a closet. When you need a small hostess, thank-you, or cheer-up gift, you'll have items on hand. A word of caution: don't buy boxes of chocolate, not because they will go bad but because on a bad day of writing, you might succumb to the urge to break them open and eat them all! —Jayne Ormerod

~*~

If you're on a tight budget, consider shopping at yard sales, consignment shops and secondhand stores. —Lesley Diehl

~*~

With several people in the house and warehouse stores selling multiple melons in a netted bag, I've found cutting melon and putting it in different size containers (like Goldilocks and the Three Bears' bowls) allows my family to eat from containers that fit their appetites and creates fewer dirty bowls. One rule: they have to finish the serving they take. I recommend containers of 1-3 cups. Teenage boys love bigger sizes. —Melinda Curtis

~*~

When I had a nine-to-five job, a family to feed, and a book to write, I often drove home at night past fast-food outlets and picked up salads. Once a week I would order hamburgers and fries. After several months of this and feeling guilty, I found a local "diet gourmet" outlet where I ordered family dinners ahead for a week. I paid more money, but saved time, plus our food was more nutritious and varied. There are always trade-offs. —Kay Kendall

~*~

Leave time to recharge yourself. The more tired you are, the longer everything takes. So try to set aside half an hour, even in a busy day, to read or watch TV. —Susan Breen

~*~

Do Christmas and birthday shopping all year long. At holiday time all you have to do is wrap. This also allows you to purchase items when you see them on sale. —Lea Wait

~*~

As a writer, my time is precious, and I don't always get to read. So I figured out a way to still be able to read while I'm multitasking. I download audiobooks onto my Kindle. I carry the Kindle with me while I'm doing chores or going for a walk and listen to the books I wouldn't otherwise have time to read. —Elizabeth Rose

~*~

When I'm involved in writing a book, life outside my office tends to take a back seat. I save time by shopping online, including grocery shopping. —Lynette Sofras

~*~

Swim laps. Sure, it takes time, but you'd be surprised at the amount of dialogue, description, and character development that comes to you when you're swimming back and forth in what amounts to a sensory deprivation chamber. This early morning aerobic exercise also charges me with lots of energy to tackle the day. —Carol Goodman Kaufman

~*~

Buy birthday and special occasion cards for the upcoming month to save trips to the store, or purchase a variety pack of greeting cards to have on hand. —Maureen Bonatch

~*~

Time often flies quickly when you browse in stores. Set a timer on your phone before entering the store. Leave when the timer goes off. This trick works especially well in bookstores where you can lose hours. —Lisa Q. Mathews

# About the Editor

*USA Today* bestselling and award-winning author Lois Winston writes mystery, romance, romantic suspense, chick lit, women's fiction, children's chapter books, and nonfiction under her own name and her Emma Carlyle pen name. *Kirkus Reviews* dubbed her critically acclaimed Anastasia Pollack Crafting Mystery series, "North Jersey's more mature answer to Stephanie Plum." In addition, Lois is an award-winning craft and needlework designer who often draws much of her source material for both her characters and plots from her experiences in the crafts industry.

Website: www.loiswinston.com
Blog: www.anastasiapollack.blogspot.com
Twitter: www.twitter.com/Anasleuth
Pinterest: www.pinterest.com/anasleuth

To receive updates on new releases and be eligible for giveaways, sign up for Lois' newsletter:
www.myauthorbiz.com/ENewsletter.php?acct=LW2467152513

# AUTHOR INDEX

Alber, Lisa, 143
Allder, Reggi, 145
Alter, Judy, 7
Ames, Krista, 35
Anderson, Rose, 59
Arnold, Cori, 113
Baker, Judy, 61
Bateman, Beverley, 95
Bell, Donnell Ann, 8
Benson, Paula Gail, 62
Bock, Kris, 64
Bonatch, Maureen, 10
Bradley, Ava, 66
Breen, Susan, 147
Bushloper, Lida, 97
Butler, Michelle Markey, 149
Chase, Ashlyn, 12
Copek, Judy, 68
Corrigan, Maya, 36
Cruz, Mariposa, 151
Curtis, Melinda, 69
Diehl, Lesley A., 115
Douglas, Conda, 152
Eady, Nancy, 70
Fairfax, Helena, 38
Faye, Jennifer, 117
Fitzpatrick, Flo, 119
Frazier, Kit, 72
Freydont, Shelley, 40
Gabrielle, Mariana, 154
Genova, Rosie, 42
Graff, Marni, 13
Guidoccio, Joanne, 99
Hamilton, Margaret S., 100
Hayden, L.C., 120
Hengerer, Linda Gordon, 74
Hiestand, Heather, 156
James, R. Franklin, 122
Jane, Kathryn, 101
Jaye, M.M., 157
John, Elizabeth, 15
Juba, Stacy, 17
Juliana, Gemma, 124
Kaufman, Carol Goodman, 98
Keir, Melissa, 18
Kendall, Kay, 76

Kennedy, A.R., 77
Kinnaman, Lynn, 103
Laval, Marie, 78
Lawson, B.V., 105
Lefeve, Claudia, 80
Loweecey, Alice, 126
Luhrs, Cynthia, 127
Masters, Sandra, 19
Mathews, Lisa Q., 82
Maurer, J.M., 21
McGregor, Sandra, 129
McIntosh, Kathy, 158
Murray, Claire A., 160
Myers, Ann, 162
Neale, Tara, 44
Netzel, Stacey Joy, 130
Ormerod, Jayne, 131
Orr, Alice, 47
Peterson, Irene, 23
Peterson, Laurel, 49
Phillips, Pepper, 132
Pineiro, Caridad, 25
Quick, Kathryn, 164
Reynolds, Renée, 51
Riviera, Josie, 27
Rose, Elizabeth, 106
Rowland, C.A., 28
Sample, Cindy, 84
Scott, Sharleen, 85
Shames, Terry, 166
Shea, Susan C., 134
Sheluk, Judy Penz, 53
Slan, Joanna Campbell, 87
Smith, Karen Rose, 30
Sofras, Lynette, 88
Spencer, Kaye, 136
Taylor, Skye, 90
Venard, Lourdes, 138
Wait, Lea, 108
Walker, Regan, 109
Winston, Lois, 54
Wynne, Aubrey, 31

www.ingramcontent.com/pod-product-compliance
Lightning Source LLC
Chambersburg PA
CBHW031641040426
42453CB00006B/172